The Courage to Succeed

Discover and Achieve What Matters Most

(and tell everything else to take a hike)

Lon W. Schiffbauer, Ph.D.

Smith & McQuarrie

Published by Smith & McQuarrie

Salt Lake City, UT

Copyright © 2016 by Lon W. Schiffbauer

Cover design, illustrations, and text design by Lon W. Schiffbauer

PRINTING HISTORY

First Edition. First printing. 01E01P07012016

ISBN: 978-0-9976961-0-3

For Susan

TABLE OF CONTENTS

Acknowledgements. 9

Introduction. 11

Chapter 1: Beware **15**

Busy vs. Productive. 17

The Purpose of This Book 21

    Is This Book for You?. 21

Chapter 2: How We Got Here. **23**

No One to Blame but Ourselves 24

    We Want to Have It All 24

    The Paradox of Abundance. 25

    Profit Motive. 25

    The Irony of Wealth. 26

    The Fear of Missing Out 27

    It's Hard to Say No 28

    The Perception of Busy vs. Idle 29

    It's a Place to Hide 29

    We Like It 30

How You Can Take It Back 31

The ADEPT Model 32

    Accept (the economics of performing with intent). 33

    Discover (what really matters) 34

    Eliminate (what doesn't matter). 35

    Plan (what matters) 36

    Take Action (with intent) 37

Benefits of Following the ADEPT Model 38

Chapter 3: Accept **45**

The Three Economic Laws of Performing with Intent 47

    1. Supply Is Finite 48

    2. Demand Is Infinite 52

    3. Resources Must Be Allocated Wisely 56

Chapter 4: Discover **65**

You Create Your Own Purpose and Meaning 67

Why Meaning Is So Important 71

The Five Steps to Distilling Priorities 76

    1. Guiding Principles 76

    2. Passion 84

    3. Strengths and Weaknesses 92

    4. Support from Others 100

    5. Supporting Infrastructure 107

Chapter 5: Eliminate **117**

Recognize 119

Resign 126

Take Charge 132

    1. Eliminate Distractions 132

    2. Beware of Scope Creep 135

    3. Don't Make a Career Out of a Task 137

    4. Beware of Bring-Me-a-Rock Exercises 138

    5. Beware of the Foot-in-the-Door Effect 138

Eliminate and Prioritize 143

Chapter 6: Plan **149**

The Benefits of Planning 151

Mapping the Journey 152

1. Your North Star – Your Why 153

2. Your Path – Your How. 158

3. Your Destination – Your Long-Term Objective. 164

4. Your Milestones – Your Short-Term Objectives 170

5. Your Steps – Your Progress Indicators 176

Putting It All Together 182

To-Do Lists and Journaling 189

How I Use My Journal. 192

Chapter 7: Take Action **203**

1. Create Purposeful Habits. 205

2. Schedule a Buffer. 212

3. Keep Your Supporters Cheering 218

4. Abandon the Myth of Multitasking 226

5. Strive for Progress; Not Perfection 230

6. Embrace the Serenity Prayer 234

7. Learn From Your Failures 244

8. Beware of Overload and Anxiety 253

9. Keep it All in Perspective. 260

10. Enjoy the Journey 267

Chapter 8: Conclusion. **273**

References **277**

ACKNOWLEDGEMENTS

Anything good I know I learned from someone else.

There is simply no way to recognize all those who have contributed to this book. The reference section alone lists some of the best minds that have addressed the topics I explore in these pages. Without the considerable work of those who have come before me, nothing here would be worth reading.

There are also many close to me who have played a vital role in this funky exercise we call "writing a book." I owe a great deal to all those who shared their personal stories with me—and in turn allowed me the privilege of sharing them with you. Many of these stories are deeply personal and have the potential to teach us valuable lessons as we explore our own potential.

I'm extremely thankful to my early readers; those intrepid few who volunteered their valuable time to help make this material fit for public consumption. Over and over, these brave souls fell on the sword of awful writing, poorly conceived concepts, and incoherent babbling to help distill from the mess something clear and accessible.

A heartfelt thank-you to my good friend and business partner, Penny Bivens. Penny in fact has prominent standing in all the categories listed above. Generous with her stories, her insights, her perspectives, and her unwavering and unselfish encouragement, Penny is as much a part of this book as any person can be.

And of course, thank you to my dear wife Susan, to whom this book is dedicated. What can I say about this amazing woman without gushing? Her support and encouragement—not to mention her promptings to get to work and finish this darn thing once and for all—have been invaluable to me. Writing this guide has taken time away from the family and my other responsibilities—time that Susan freely gave up without complaint because she knew this work was important to me.

Finally, thank *you*, dear reader, for giving this book a chance to help you in your life's journey. Does music exist without an audience? Is there such a thing as art if no one gazes upon the canvas? And does a book exist if no one reads it? There isn't an author alive who doesn't hope someone will pick up his or her book and find something of value within its pages. Life is a marvelous and wondrous thing, just waiting for us to do something great. If I can help you along that path then it would be my privilege.

INTRODUCTION

So here's the deal: I was supposed to be an oceanographer.

When I was six years old I was watching TV with my father. On the screen an aquatic superhero, clad in black scuba gear, floated suspended in the sea. Then a great dark mass emerged into view. It was an enormous whale, strong and beautiful in its indifference. If the whale noticed the diver, it gave no indication. By contrast, the narrator paid unmatched homage to the beast. In his thick French accent he called the whale such things as, "the great denizen of the sea," "lord of the depths," and other titles reserved for things of myth and legend. His slow and careful voice betrayed a profound reverence for the whale, a tone perfectly suited for addressing royalty.   *deep respect*

With my eyes glued to the flickering screen, I reached back and tugged on my father's pant leg. "Dad? What's that man's job?"

My father looked over long enough to glance at the screen. "He's an oceanographer," he told me.

With more earnest intent than should ever be heard from a child my age, I told my father that I was going to be an oceanographer.

Whether he recognized the steel in my words wasn't clear, but it didn't matter. The moment had been indelibly etched in my psyche. From that time forth, no other childhood memory existed.

My newly-discovered purpose became an obsession. Over the next few years I lived in the library, reading every book on oceanography and marine biology I could lay my hands on. I drew more pictures of dolphins and whales than had previously existed in the canon of human history. By the time I was in school I knew more about the oceans and all they contained than most adults. I joined Greenpeace and became a supreme pest, evangelizing the cause of the oceans to anyone who would listen. I saved my allowance and had a sweatshirt custom made with the words "SAVE THE WHALES" ironed on in big felt letters. I learned French, even going so far as to spend a year in Paris and attending a French public school so I could one day work with Jacques Cousteau. Such is the logic of a youthful mind.   *French naval officer, explorer, conservationist, scientist...*

Everything was moving along swimmingly, or so I thought. But really it was nothing more than a child's flight of fancy. For all the effort I invested, little of it was directed in a meaningful way toward my ultimate goal. I mean come on— *French*? How was *that* going to help me become an oceanographer? It would have been better had I spent a summer doing crap work on a research vessel,

1) inhabitant : resident   / 2) in a way that can't be removed / 3) human soul

but that's not how the dreamer's mind works. And therein lies the problem. A dream isn't a plan, and in the absence of a plan we become easily distracted. In truth by the time I was 17 I was no closer to by goal than the day I uttered my ultimatum. This left me very vulnerable to the minefield of life.

In time my interest in oceanography waned. There were many reasons for this, but most notably was that I struggled as a student. In hindsight I see now that I had failed to develop proper study habits and dedicate the requisite time and energy to my studies, but as a kid I didn't understand this. All I knew was I wasn't a very successful student, and the only reason I could come up with was that I must have been slow, of below-average intelligence. As hard as it was for me to come to grips with this, it was nothing compared with the realization that then followed:

Oceanographers are scientists, and scientists are smart. *Really* smart.

When I realized this a little part of me died inside. I felt I was unequal to the challenge and so abandoned my dream.

No matter how much we want something, it's nothing more than a dream if we don't have a plan. We don't achieve our dreams by accident. Oh we may be busy as all get out, chasing our ambitions, learning French and whatnot, but we shouldn't confuse motion with progress. As it's been said, a rocking horse is a busy little critter, but it never gets anywhere. A plan allows us to set a single goal ahead of all others, chart a deliberate course toward that goal, launch our ships, and stave off the sirens' songs of self-doubt, confused priorities, and other challenges that would steer us off course.

Finding Your Treasure

We all know that when searching for buried treasure, 'X' marks the spot, but we may not always know what our treasure is. Or maybe we do know what our 'X' is but are unsure how to begin our journey—or even find the courage to do so. Striking out on such an adventure can seem daunting, after all.

This book is all about turning our dreams into plans, our plans into actions, and our actions into meaningful results. This is done through the ADEPT Model, a guiding philosophy and structured process by which we can identify and achieve those things that give us meaning and purpose.

The elements of the ADEPT Model are far from revolutionary. Those familiar with Peter Drucker and his principles of Management by Objectives (MBO) will detect his DNA.[1] Fans of Stephen Covey will find themselves smiling at

1) Break in, smash in

an old friend, as will adherents of Joseph Campbell, Patrick Lencioni, Simon Sinek, Brené Brown, Viktor Frankl, and Monty Python. (Hey, I call truth where I see it, baby.) Principles associated with strategic business planning, SWOT analyses, and personality profiles also make an appearance. It's not my intent or desire to pass the ADEPT Model off as something that will put all other works to shame. Far from it. Many greats have gone before me; this model simply stands on their shoulders. As I tell my college students, you already know everything we're going to discuss; my job is simply to help you understand what you already know. By understanding, we can better appreciate and implement what works.

So what's different about the ADEPT Model? First, as I mentioned, it draws upon a considerable amount of current organizational and behavioral psychological research, including the works of dozens of business leaders, psychologists, economists, professors, ethicists, writers, lecturers—people who have dedicated their lives to helping us understand how to accomplish great things. By considering these many perspectives we'll be able to develop a deeper, multi-dimensional perspective of how we can succeed in whatever we set out to achieve.

Second, the model offers a very clear and easy-to-follow process whereby we can understand what's most important and then go after it. Many works today offer valuable insights into what it means to perform with intent, but precious few offer a process that we can easily adopt and implement. I developed the ADEPT Model with this guiding principle in mind: provide a step-by-step process that we can implement today—and see results almost immediately.

Finally, I wanted to offer a model that was both thorough and yet accessible. Lately I feel like there are really only two options available to us when it comes to books on self-improvement: the short fluff fable that barely lasts a plane flight, or the exhaustive tome—a book so long that if I had the time to read and assimilate the entire thing I wouldn't need advice on how to better manage my time. Both extremes have their place, but I wanted to develop something that filled the middle ground.

My Role in Your Journey

As you can see, I have grand intentions for this book, but intentions are meaningless. Your performance is all that matters. You see, the operative word in the phrase *self-help book* is *self*. It's all up to you. You're the master of your own journey. If I can help you along the way, then wonderful. I'd like to think my education, research, and life experiences have taught me a thing or two that can help others, but ultimately we are all our own guides. Consider this: I chose the title *The Courage to Succeed* because while we all strive after success in some way or another, we sometimes lack the intestinal fortitude to go "all in" as it were and really go after what matters. I believe the principles and practices contained within these pages will help you succeed in accomplishing what you decide is most important, but that doesn't change the fact that it's up to you. You are the actor; you are the decider; you are the one that will determine if you achieve amazing things or settle for something that is less than your potential. Living the mediocre life takes little courage; living a full life directed toward what matters takes tremendous daring. Mind you, I'm not confused; the most successful lives or enterprises have many non-successes (yep—failures) threaded throughout them. This book will help you map your journey toward success, as well as navigate the treacherous waters that no doubt await. In the end my hope is to help get you where you want to go—someplace incredible— but the road is yours to travel.

Oh, and before I leave, that oceanography dream of mine? Let's just say that I'm the king of reinvention. I've been on this planet half a century and I figure I still have another three or four good decades in me. So the next time we meet, ask me how I'm doing with regards to my oceanography career. See if I've moved it from a dream to a plan. One day I'll be able to smile and show you my map.

CHAPTER 1: BEWARE
(the barrenness of a busy life)

It is not enough to be industrious; so are the ants. What are you industrious about?

– Henry David Thoreau
American author, philosopher, social critic, historian

Consider the plate spinner. You know who I'm talking about. He's the guy who spins saucers on poles while *Sabre Dance* plays in the background. He keeps the dinnerware precariously suspended, just moments away from utter catastrophe. The performer starts out with four or five plates, and while the trick is impressive, he's calm, cool, and collected. Then he adds a sixth, then a seventh. Still he's coping well enough, but you start to notice that some of the plates are dangerously close to toppling. Then in the nick of time our performer dashes over and gives them another quick spin. Despite this he finds time to add an eighth, ninth, even a tenth plate. Now the man is racing about like a caffeinated squirrel, working furiously to keep all the saucers suspended. Clearly the dishes are struggling against the power of sweet gravity. So what does the man do? That's right, he adds more plates! What in the world is he thinking? By now all grace and decorum has left the stage. He's sliding to and fro, tripping over own feet, all while saucers wobble their last feeble death throws. Finally the inevitable happens. One of the plates goes crashing to the floor. Undeterred, our friend replaces the saucer with a new one and sets it spinning, as though the fate of this plate is somehow different from that of its predecessor. But it isn't. In time our performer loses the battle, the plates tumble and shatter into a thousand pieces, and that's entertainment.

In our own way, we're all plate spinners.

In this hectic modern age we're pulled in so many directions it's like being drawn and quartered. At work we have deadlines to meet, assignments to deliver, and meetings to attend. We run this way and that, reporting to our various supervisors, project managers, stakeholders, customers—all demanding their pound of flesh. Once at home we drive our kids all over creation for school, music lessons, sports, dance, and anything else we can think of. There's homework to do, fundraisers to organize, supplies to purchase, teachers to meet, and recitals to attend. It never ends. Work and home are not the only fiends taxing our time and energy. We feel our bodies falling apart in all this stress, so we commit to exercising more and to eating right. But where's the time to run, bike, or hit the gym? Then there's our spiritual and emotional needs to consider. We want to be good members of our communities so we find opportunities to volunteer, maybe at schools, libraries, religious institutions, or community centers. We participate in fun runs, work on whatever project awaits us in the garage, create art, write blogs, remodel the home, or work in the garden, always wishing there were more hours in the day. Marketers tell us we need to buy more, consume more. Politicians and social causes contentiously attempt to rile our indignation and spur us to action. There's social media, that insatiable beast that must be continuously fed. Emails, texts, and phone calls vie for our attention. Notifications on our smart phones sing out. Lights, chimes, vibrations—alerts telling us to drop whatever we're doing and give them our undivided attention. And yet, no matter how much we do, we always seem to be behind. It's all part of a zero-sum-game.

These are all the plates we work to keep from crashing to the ground. We think to ourselves, "It shouldn't be like this. I shouldn't be so harried and stressed," but we don't know what to do about it. So we continue on, spinning the endless plates until we lose our sanity. No wonder Socrates warned us, "Beware the barrenness of the busy life."

Speaking for myself, I don't believe our lives were meant to be so frantic and chaotic. (Yeah, so this is the philosopher in me talking, but indulge me.) I like to think the aspirational faculties afforded us by these great big melon-sized brains we possess were intended for more than the pedestrian task of corporal survival. Our lives can be so much more—should we allow them to be. We're not just survivors; we're artists and poets, philosophers and theologians, musicians and engineers, humanitarians and scientists, explorers and inventors—thinkers and doers of extraordinary things. The busy and hectic life stands against these higher causes—or at least threatens to if not watched carefully.

BUSY VS. PRODUCTIVE

With all this going on in our lives, we must be tremendously productive, right? We work late, sleep little, eat at our desks, and multitask unceasingly. We spend every minute of every day seeing to some responsibility, whether it be work, family, community, or school. So how can we *not* be productive?

The problem is we've come to confuse *busy* with *productive*. We run back and forth between our commitments, keeping each one alive on little more than a saline drip, but then fail to really deliver on anything in a meaningful way. Our efforts are scattered and poorly directed. Instead of getting all the wood behind the arrow, we diffuse our time and energy across disparate commitments, some with little to no importance. It's what Bruch and Ghoshal call "unproductive or mindless busy-ness" or "active nonaction."[1]

Another way we confuse *busy* with *productive* is by focusing on *activities* over *results*, something Stephen Covey the younger talks about in his book, *The Speed of Trust*.[2] Exercising is an *activity*, but losing weight and getting fit are the *results*. When we focus on the activity we fail to hold ourselves accountable for the results. We often make frenetic action its own reward. Consequently, we don't have to examine the outcome in the cold hard light of day. "I'm busy," we tell ourselves, "therefore I'm successful." No further inquiry is necessary or even welcome.

We see this every day. Take the workplace, for example. The 40-hour workweek has become urban legend. Research suggests that over 25 million American workers put in 49 or more hours a week.[3] Over ten million Americans spend 60 hours or more at work.[4] A Gallup survey performed in 2014 substantiated these figures, stating that the average American worker logged 46.7 hours a week, nearly a full extra eight-hour workday. Only about 40 percent of those surveyed reported working the standard 40-hour workweek. What's perhaps more astonishing is to see the percentage of Americans who work 50 to 59 hours a week—about 21 percent. Those who work 60 hours or greater accounted for a staggering 18 percent![5]

Now all these extra hours might be fine if we were all working purposefully, but we're not. According to Bruch and Ghoshal, few of us have figured out how to perform with intent.[6] To help describe the nature of this problem, these researchers identified four quadrants along two axes. The vertical axis is *focus*— our ability to apply concentrated attention to a task. When we're wholly zeroed in on a task to the exclusion of all else we're focused. The horizontal axis is *personal investment* (or *energy* as Bruch and Ghoshal called it), the vigor and intense personal commitment we bring to a task. When we're intrinsically motivated to excel because the task is important to us then we perform with energy and passion, investing of ourselves because we see the goal as worthy of our best efforts.

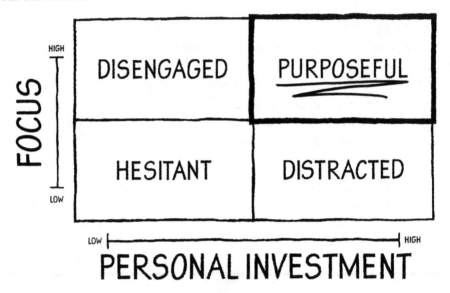

Depending on our level of focus and personal investment, we may find ourselves in one of four quadrants:

► **Hesitant:** With little focus or personal investment, the *Hesitant* (or the *Procrastinators*, as Bruch and Ghoshal called them) struggle to take the initiative, raise the level of performance, or engage in anything in a meaningful way. They'll perform routine tasks like attend meetings, write emails, do the laundry, clean the house, or do any other perfunctory thing required of them, but they'll fail to do anything with passion and energy.

Consider the fable of the eagle who thought he was a chicken. One day a farmer found an abandoned eagle's egg. To see what would happen he slipped the egg under a brooding hen with her other eggs. When the egg hatched the mother hen raised the chick as one of her own. Thinking he was a chicken, the baby eaglet walked, clucked, scratched, and pecked like the other chicks. Eventually he grew and became a great beautiful eagle, yet he continued to behave like a chicken

One day another eagle flew down and asked what on earth his fellow bird of prey was doing, down on the ground, scratching among the chickens.

"What do you mean?" the grounded eagle asked, "I *am* a chicken. Leave me alone."

The *Hesitant* are the baby eaglets, unwilling to rise up to their full potential, preferring instead to play it safe and scratch out a living among the chickens. These are people who watch with envy as others excel, take the initiative, maybe even start their own business or set big personal goals. Yet they hang back, lacking the focus or personal investment necessary to rise up and act. To protect their own egos they ridicule and mock those who dare to set such ambitious goals. They may even hope to see them fail, thereby validating their own hesitation. A little taste of schadenfreude.

▶ **Disengaged:** The *Disengaged* have a great deal of focus but lack the intrinsic motivation to really excel. While they focus on the job at hand, their commitment is halfhearted and uninspired. The *Disengaged* are those who dutifully go about mundane tasks—tasks that give them neither purpose nor meaning. They watch the clock, mark the days off the calendar, and think of nothing but their next vacation. They're very focused on what they're doing, only they're not inspired.

When I was a child I was intrigued by a clever little novelty called the drinking or dipping bird. (Google it; it's awesome.) Shaped like a fat thermometer with a bird's head and a top hat, it rocked back and forth as it drank from a glass of water. Over and over, like a perpetual motion machine, it dipped and rocked, dipped and rocked, dipped and rocked. Oh sure, it was fascinating at first, but eventually I got bored and so set off in search of my next distraction. Yet the bird continued to dip and rock, as it had when there was an audience. Despite the absence of onlookers it soldiered on, over and over, ceaselessly fulfilling its function, all without any real purpose.

▶ **Distracted:** The *Distracted* are those with intense personal commitment to the work but little focus to help direct that effort. These are the plate spinners: energetic and well-intentioned people who confuse frenetic motion with constructive action. They want to have it all, to leave no stone unturned, to chase after every opportunity that comes their way, fearing that failure to do so may result in future loss and regret. These are they who wear their hectic chaotic schedules on their chests as a red badge of courage; a symbol of their perceived self-importance and superior work ethic. With alligator tears they complain ceaselessly about how busy they are, asserting in their passive-aggressive way that they're oh so more important and in-demand than the rest of us. Yet despite all the bravado they have remarkably little to show for their efforts.

▸ **Purposeful:** The minority—that elite group we want to join—is the *Purposeful* category. As we'll see, it's one thing to perform; it's another to do so with purposeful intent. A dog chasing its tail is actively engaged in the activity—is performing—but without intent and purpose it's simply wasting energy. Those who perform with intent are highly-motivated and focused on what really matters. They enjoy a clarity of purpose that helps them make sound decisions, prioritize their time, and pick their battles for maximum effect. No doubt those in this quadrant are *busy*. What makes them *productive* is the singled-minded focus they bring to a goal that has purpose and meaning for them. These people know the difference between *busy* and *productive*.

If *Purposeful* is our ultimate goal then we need to figure out how to get from whatever quadrant we currently occupy to the sweet, sweet real-estate of *Purposeful*. For instance, moving from *Hesitant* to *Purposeful* takes courage, even the willingness to fail without losing heart. In a powerful speech delivered in Paris in 1910, Theodore Roosevelt offered these words to embolden those looking for the courage to take risks and strive to do great things:

> "It is not the critic who counts; not the man who points out how the strong man stumbles, or where the doer of deeds could have done them better. The credit belongs to the man who is actually in the arena, whose face is marred by dust and sweat and blood; who strives valiantly; who errs, who comes short again and again, because there is no effort without error and shortcoming; but who does actually strive to do the deeds; who knows great enthusiasms, the great devotions; who spends himself in a worthy cause; who at the best knows in the end the triumph of high achievement, and who at the worst, if he fails, at least fails while daring greatly, so that his place shall never be with those cold and timid souls who neither know victory nor defeat." [7]

For those of us in the *Disengaged* box, moving to *Purposeful* requires us to discover what rouses our intrinsic motivators. Moving from *Distracted* to *Purposeful* asks us to let go of all the ways society affirms the mythos of the busy individual and instead focus on the ends rather than the means.

THE PURPOSE OF THIS BOOK

The purpose of this book is simple: to help us find the courage, focus, and intrinsic motivation we need to accomplish great and marvelous things— things that have purpose and meaning in our lives. As stated earlier, it's about turning our dreams into plans, our plans into actions, and our actions into meaningful results. This book is not necessarily about how to be less busy; rather, it's about how to be more productive. It's not about how to make more money; it's about how to be more accomplished. It's about learning to recognize the sirens of legend who beckon us to esteem the scurrying busy life over a life dedicated to producing with intent. Ultimately, it's about ridding ourselves of those meaningless activities that give us the illusion of productivity but in the end merely distract us from what really matters.

Is This Book for You?

This book is for the plate spinners; those who feel they're scrambling this way and that, keeping things from shattering into smithereens but never able to accomplish anything meaningful. It's for those who are too busy dealing with fire drills to take any time to map out a strategic path to meaningful success.

This book can also help the dipping birds; those who feel as though they're merely going through the motions, doing whatever needs to be done, day in and day out, yet are unable to shake the thought that nothing they're doing has any real meaning or purpose.

Likewise, this book can help the grounded eagles, scraping out a living among the chickens; those who have big dreams but are uncertain where to begin. It's for those who want to reinvent themselves but are struggling to find the courage to take that first step.

It doesn't matter whether you're a company executive or an in-the-trenches employee, a student or a soccer mom, an inventor or an entrepreneur, a business owner or a volunteer. If anything I've said so far resonates with you, this book is for you. If you want to enjoy a greater sense of fulfillment and satisfaction in what you do, no matter your field of endeavor, this books is for you. If you want to wake up in the morning with a sense of excitement and adventure for what the day has in store, and go to bed knowing that your contributions made a difference, this book is for you.

If at this point you're still reading, odds are this book is for you.

CHAPTER 2: HOW WE GOT HERE
(and how to we can take it back)

We are taught you must blame your father, your sisters, your brothers, the school, the teachers, but never blame yourself. It's never your fault. But it's always your fault, because if you wanted to change you're the one who has got to change.

– Katharine Hepburn
American actress

The absurd pace at which we try to be everywhere and do everything is crazy and unsustainable. We know this, and yet we keep doing it. Why is that? Why do we add more and more plates to our stage?

It's tempting to be fatalistic here and say that such is the human condition; that life requires us to run breathlessly from one obligation to the next, giving just enough of our time and energy to keep it from toppling, but not so much as to cause other responsibilities to crumble from neglect. It's just the way things are, right? We're heinously busy and there's nothing we can do about it.

To be sure, life can be a harsh taskmaster. I've been around long enough to know that the Buddhist tenet that life is suffering isn't too far off the mark. That said, I believe this fatalistic stance incorrectly shifts the blame away from us. Let me show you what I mean.

NO ONE TO BLAME BUT OURSELVES

It's tempting to feel powerless against the oncoming tide as we survey the vast numbers of those who would have us do their bidding. The thing is, we really have no one to blame but ourselves. On one hand this may sound like a stern chastisement, but there's another way of looking at it. The fact that we're living in cages of our own construction means we can get out of them as well. All we need is the courage to do so—courage, and an understanding of how we got here in the first place. Here are some thoughts to consider:

We Want to Have It All

We want it all, and who can blame us? Life is pretty darn exciting and there's so much to experience, explore, and become. We want to have a family and a career. We want time to pursue our interests, maybe take a class or earn a degree. There are community and charitable causes we want to support. We want toys—things like boats, vacation homes, craft rooms, workshops—and the time to enjoy these luxuries. There's so much to be had, experienced, and enjoyed; it's hard to draw the line.

The problem is that this need to have it all takes a toll on us. For example, a recent study suggests that middle-class working mothers are driving themselves to exhaustion as they try to have a career while at the same time provide their school children with extra-curricular activities every day of the week.[1] And mothers aren't the only ones who want to have it all. Increasingly fathers are feeling the tug-of-war between career and family. The majority of fathers surveyed reported that fatherhood was their number-one priority and that they wished they had more time to spend at home.[2] However, at the same time both men and women are loath to give up time and effort in the workplace— investments that could spell career opportunities and greater prosperity for themselves and their families. And that's not all. We want time alone, to read, to be with those close to us, or to simply to recharge. As Mary Chapin Carpenter says in her song *Passionate Kisses*:

> *Is it too much to ask*
> *I want a comfortable bed that won't hurt my back*
> *Food to fill me up*
> *And warm clothes and all that stuff*
>
> ...

Is it too much to demand
I want a full house and a rock and roll band
Pens that won't run out of ink
And cool quiet and time to think

…

Do I want too much
Am I going overboard to want that touch
I shout it out to the night
"Give me what I deserve, 'cause it's my right!" [3]

"It's my right?!" That's some pretty heavy-duty we-want-to-have-it-all stuff right there, Mary!

The Paradox of Abundance

The overwhelming abundance of choices available to us has made it increasingly difficult to make what feels like the right choice. When we have only two choices, narrowing down the best option is pretty straight-forward. Heck, even if we were to close our eyes and chose one at random, we'd have a 50/50 chance of being right. And if both options are viable—which is to say there's no clear right or wrong choice—then we pretty much can't lose. But when we have hundreds of options to choose from, selecting the "right" one becomes an exercise in statistical analytics. We take even the smallest decisions very seriously because we feel our nuanced choices reflect who we are. One study suggests that when people are presented with ten or more choices they make poorer decisions.[4] Every day we dedicate vast amounts of cognitive resources to working through the minutia of our choices, and for very little return. Yet today there are more and more acclaimed television shows that need watching, more books to read, more skills to develop and improve, more new diets to try, and so on. All of this creates pressure on us to avoid choosing and instead chase after them all.

Profit Motive

In his famous work, *An Inquiry into the Nature and Causes of the Wealth of Nations*, Adam Smith states that, "Every individual who employs his capital in the support of domestic industry, necessarily endeavours so to direct that industry that its produce may be of the greatest possible value."[5] Translated for those of us not educated in 18th-century Scotland, when we invest our resources, such as time and money, we naturally want to get the greatest return possible from that investment. Put another way, the profit motive drives us to engage in activities that are intended to increase profit and wealth.

So what does this mean for our busy schedules? It means that culturally we have been trained to view industry as the root of all wealth and prosperity, and that seeking after this wealth is a noble and virtuous thing. As Smith puts it:

> "*Labour was the first price, the original purchase—money that was paid for all things. It was not by gold or by silver, but by labour, that all the wealth of the world was originally purchased; and its value, to those who possess it, and who want to exchange it for some new productions, is precisely equal to the quantity of labour which it can enable them to purchase or command.*" [6]

Labor is what provides wealth, and the more labor one performs, the greater the monetary reward. Simply put, we see busy-ness as the path to riches. With this as our underlying assumption it's no wonder we're so busy! Of course this may very well be the case, but most of us are spreading our busy-ness quotient too broadly to always have the desired monetary effect.

The Irony of Wealth

We have this image that wealth erases the need to work, but ironically, wealth often creates work. For example, you may have heard the saying, "The two happiest days of my life were the day I bought my boat and the day I sold it." Boats are a lot of work to keep up, license, and house. Then of course now that we've made that considerable investment we feel obligated to use the blasted thing. But finding the time to get away and tool around the lake can be pretty difficult. Even if we do get out there, odds are good we'll be checking our email and social media half the time. The stress created by being away from everything practically negates any enjoyment or relaxation we may hope to receive.

A friend of mine bought a cabin up in the mountains. A beautiful thing. Now every winter all he can think about is the pipes bursting. Then come spring he gets the mice infestations. Then there are the community fees, the upkeep, and all that good stuff. Now don't get me wrong, it's a wonderful place and he enjoys getting away now and again, but with so little time and with no cell phone coverage up there, he doesn't get away as often as he would like. Nevertheless, he's a slave to this thing that was intended to provide leisure.

The Fear of Missing Out

This one is so pervasive that it has its own acronym—FOMO. We can see FOMO in two ways:

▶ Our desire to stay continually connected with what others are doing.[7]

▶ Our fear that by saying *no* to an opportunity we may in some way be slamming the door on something that could one day change our lives for the better.

We've all heard stories of people who had the opportunity to make an obscene amount of money but for some reason or another missed the window. Atari founder Nolan Bushnell turned down the chance to invest $50,000 in Apple back when the company was first starting up. Had Bushnell invested he would have owned a third of Apple, worth billions today.[8] Ronald Wayne, Apple's third co-founder, didn't fare much better. He sold his ten percent stake in the company for $800 two weeks after the launch. These days a ten percent stake would be worth tens of billions of dollars.[9] Companies like Facebook and Google have similar histories floating about. Joe Green, Mark Zuckerberg's college roommate, turned down an offer to help create Facebook in exchange for a stake in the company that would have been worth something in the neighborhood of $400 million today.[10] On the Google front, David Cowan, a partner at Bessemer Venture Partners, had the opportunity to back the venture when it was young. According to the company's "anti-portfolios" (a fun and self-deprecating look at missed opportunities), "Cowan's college friend rented her garage to Sergey and Larry for their first year. In 1999 and 2000 she tried to introduce Cowan to 'these two really smart Stanford students writing a search engine.' Students? A new search engine? In the most important moment ever for Bessemer's anti-portfolio, Cowan asked her, 'How can I get out of this house without going anywhere near your garage?'"[11] James Altucher is another venture capitalist who took a pass on Google, turning down the opportunity to buy 20 percent of the company for about $1 million, which today would have equaled tens of billions.[12]

Because we're afraid of missing out we have a hard time saying *no* to anything, no matter how small or insignificant. FOMO is especially observable when it comes to mobile phones, texting, and social media. We live in a constant state of anxiety that somewhere others are having rewarding experiences, and that by being absent we're missing out.[13] As a result our mobile devices are rarely out of arm's reach (indeed, if ever out of our hands). Most of those talking on their cell phones or texting while driving aren't putting the final touches on a nuclear disarmament treaty with North Korea or talking a doctor through a life-saving surgical procedure. They're assuaging their fear of missing out, of the anxiety they feel when they're not connected to the office, their families, or friends.

The problem is that FOMO reduces our focus on the things that really matter. The cosmos doesn't know what matters so it feeds us opportunities from every direction. It's up to us to evaluate and accept the opportunities that make the most sense and discard those that don't. But how can we tell which ones make sense? Little events today can have a huge effect tomorrow, and vice-versa. FOMO feeds off of this uncertainty and tells us that every opportunity, no matter how small, should be explored.

It's Hard to Say No

It's not always easy to say *no* when someone asks us for something. Sometimes it feels downright impossible, like we're obligated to say *yes*, regardless of what it might mean for the rest of our commitments. We're generally hardwired to please. We all have a need to establish close personal bonds and relationships with others, thereby finding emotional and caring support and security.[14]

> *"Sometimes it's difficult to separate the request from the relationship, as though saying* no *to the request is somehow saying* no *to a cherished relationship painstakingly built over many years."*

This is the case, not only in our general social interactions but in the workplace as well.[15] All this means we're desperate not to jeopardize these relationships— relationships upon which we depend to feel a sense of caring support, security, and belonging. Saying *no*, we might reason, could possibly threaten these relationships. Sometimes it's difficult to separate the request from the relationship, as though saying *no* to the request is somehow saying *no* to a cherished relationship painstakingly built over many years.[16]

Ultimately we say *yes* and *no* to many things each and every day. For every action we take (or don't take), we're making good on a promise of *yes* or *no*. However, if these promises are not grounded in clear priorities then we are at the mercy of the whims of others.[17]

The Perception of Busy vs. Idle

In his book, *The Protestant Ethic and the Spirit of Capitalism*, Max Weber coined the phrase "puritan work ethic" (or as it's more commonly known today, "protestant work ethic")[18] In creating this term, Weber argued that Protestant Christians (especially the Calvinists) were particularly energetic in their work habits. This led to the development of capitalism and the virtue of hard work in a modern economy.[19] Few ideas have taken such hold of the Western ideal of "hard work" and "busy" as the puritan work ethic. But perhaps more importantly, the principle is founded in large part in theology and ideas of virtue. This gives the puritan work ethic enormous weight. Thanks to this principle, the idle are not merely *lazy*, they're perceived as *immoral*, lacking in virtue and character. It's of little wonder then that we don't want to be perceived as idle or unoccupied. We even go so far as to over-engineer a relatively simple task to give the impression that it's much more difficult than it really is. What's more, we require hard work from those around us. To some degree we constantly assess the level of effort others put out. The last thing we want is to have others think we're not pulling our weight, so we make sure every minute of our time is engaged. In the prologue of the *Canterbury Tales*, Geoffrey Chaucer said of the Sergeant of the Law, "Nowhere a man so busy of his class, and yet he seemed much busier than he was."[20] It seems the pious display of industry is no modern invention.

It's a Place to Hide

As Saint Francis de Sales points out, there's no better way to put off doing the big things than by busying ourselves with the little things. Busy procrastination (or as Bruch and Ghoshal might call it, "active nonaction"[21]) seems to be a great way to *look* busy without actually *being* busy. Sometimes the things that need to be done are big, daunting, ambiguous, or even unpleasant and intimidating. In these cases the busy whirl of menial activity can provide a weird sort of sanctuary. We hide behind our busy schedules, putting off those things that really should be done but for whatever reason we choose to avoid. The beauty of this strategy is that the opium of the puritan work ethic can be just enough to overcome the sense of guilt we feel for putting off what really needs to be done.

We Like It

While all these reasons hold true, the fact of the matter is we like being busy. Oh sure, we complain about it, but secretly we love it. There are good reasons for this. It provides us with a sense of accomplishment, promotes self-confidence, and fills us with a sense of competence. Speaking for myself, few things get my head straight quite as well as hard work. But there's a less wholesome aspect to being so busy. As Edward M. Hallowell puts it in his book, *Crazy Busy: Overstretched, Overbooked, and About to Snap! Strategies for Handling Your Fast-Paced Life*, being "crazy busy" inflates our sense of self-importance. If we're busy then it must stand to reason that we're in demand, and therefore important.[22] Logically then (we reason with ourselves) the busier we are the more important we are. Talk about heady stuff! This is exactly what those in the *Distracted* box love to feel.

Being busy can also act as a kind of armor, a shield that keeps us from becoming vulnerable to attack. In her New York Times bestseller, *Daring Greatly*, Dr. Brené Brown argues that people use a variety of strategies to numb themselves against the likely discomfort brought on by vulnerability. Being constantly busy is one of these strategies. Talking about her own version of '*crazy busy*', Dr. Brown says:

> "*I often say that when they start having 12-step meetings for busy-aholics, they'll need to rent out football stadiums. We are a culture of people who've bought into the idea that if we stay busy enough, the truth of our lives won't catch up with us.*"[23]

We can see it all around us. We brag about how busy we are, waving our self-perceived martyrdom syndrome for all to see and admire. We think what we do is oh so important and needs everyone's constant attention and support. We work 60-hour weeks and look upon those who don't with slight regard. We use phrases like, "I'll sleep when I'm dead" or "I don't have time to be sick" as though these vapid phrases merit praise.[24] We rush about, perpetually ten minutes late to every meeting, talking on cell phones, texting, lending half an ear in meetings, all the while congratulating ourselves for being indispensable to so many people. Drugs don't have half the power to make us feel so amazing!

HOW YOU CAN TAKE IT BACK

With so many demands placed upon us from every direction it's easy to feel like we're no longer agents unto ourselves. Instead we feel like we're being forever acted upon by others. Everyone but us seems to have claim to our time, our money, our energy, even our passions. We're told what we should do and what we should care about by employers, marketers, the news, social media, politicians, and our families. It's no wonder we often find ourselves busy as all get out but have so little to show for our efforts.

> **The greatest danger for most of us is not that our aim is too high and we miss it, but that it is too low and we reach it.**
>
> *– Michelangelo*

Thing is, we're not so powerless. In fact, we're pretty darn good at filtering out the clutter. Let me give you an example. Have you ever had a conversation with someone at a party? All around you a cacophony of conversations and background noises are vying for your attention, yet somehow you're able to block all this out and focus on the person standing in front of you. This ability is called the *cocktail party effect*, and while there are a variety of theories as to how we're able to do this, the point is that we can.[1] This is what we need to learn to do when it comes to focusing our time and attention.

We will always be surrounded by those who would distract us from what matters to us—the other voices and conversations at the cocktail party—but that doesn't mean we have to be forever at their beck and call. We can give our full attention to what matters most in our lives—that person right in front of us at the party.

If you're reading this book then odds are you're looking for a way to simplify your hectic life, figure out what really matters, and find the courage to accomplish great things. The good news is you can do all of this, and really, it's not that complicated. Mind you, "not that complicated" doesn't mean "easy." One doesn't just flip a switch and change a life. It'll take work and discipline, maybe even a little blood, sweat, and tears. …Wait! Don't close the book yet! It'll be worth it, I promise!

THE ADEPT MODEL

Adept means *highly skilled* and *completely versed in a given proficiency*. It comes from the Latin word *adeptus*, the past participle of *adipisci*. In Latin it means *to pursue and attain; to arrive at, to achieve.*[2] It's appropriate that the acronym for this model would spell out *adept*. We all want to attain a high level of skill and competence in those things that fire us up. It's by virtue of these skills that we go on to accomplish great and marvelous things. The ADEPT Model is all about helping us achieve what matters most—that which gives us the greatest sense of purpose in life.

The ADEPT Model is designed in such a way as to help us do three things: get our heads straight, focus our intentions, and turn our intentions into specific actions. It also starts with the big picture in mind, employing a sort of blue-sky thinking, then helps us work out the day-to-day nuts and bolts from there. We all know people (indeed, sometimes ourselves) who have dreams but then no idea where or how to start. As a result their dream never progresses past fantasy. Others may be very industrious but their actions are poorly directed toward a purposeful goal. Success comes from the elegant integration of dreams and plans. One without the other is a recipe for failure. The ADEPT Model understands this and provides the ballroom for these two partners to dance and show off their stuff.

So with this in mind, let me introduce you to the ADEPT Model:

Accept	Accept the three economic laws of performing with intent.
Discover	Discover what matters most and gives you meaning and purpose.
Eliminate	Eliminate what doesn't matter—things that are distracting you from your purpose.
Plan	Plan a course of action to achieving what matters.
Take Action	Take action and develop the mindset you need to accomplish great things.

Pretty simple and straight-forward, right? Yeah, what isn't? True, it's not terribly complicated, but don't let the simplicity of the model fool you. Let's look at each one of these in a little more depth.

Accept (the economics of performing with intent)

We may want to have it all, but the economic fact of the matter is we can't. Now I know this is probably generating a myriad of feelings. Intellectually we know we can't have it all, but our passions, actions, and ambitions say otherwise. While it may feel remedial—even pedantic—there are three economic laws of performing with intent that we have to accept:

1. **Supply Is Finite:** The ingredients needed to succeed—things like time, energy, money, and cognitive resources—are in limited supply. These are finite resources, and when they run out, they run out.

2. **Demand Is Infinite:** While there is a finite supply of resources, the demand for these resources is infinite. There's no end to the number of requests for our time, energy, money, and cognitive resources from all those around us, such as employers, customers, family, community, or even ourselves.

3. **Resources Must Be Allocated Wisely:** Succeed lies in our ability to wisely and deliberately allocate our finite resources so that the demand doesn't exceed the supply.

Discover (what really matters)

Everyone knows that 'X' marks the spot. For centuries (or so we imagine) treasure maps have led all who would brave the journey to the fabled 'X,' the spot where success and riches await. Great. But what if we don't know what our 'X' is? We all want to get there, but where is *there*?

Discovering what really matters means looking inside and deciding what deserves our limited resources and what, quite frankly, doesn't. The economics of performing with intent tell us we can't do everything and be successful. This means discovering what's most important to us. To do this we'll examine our:

1. **Guiding Principles:** The values that direct how we behave, what we believe, and the decisions we make, both large and small.

2. **Meaning and Purpose:** The passions that get us up in the morning and motivate us to perform and excel.

3. **Strengths and Weaknesses:** The abilities, skills, and competencies we bring to the table, as well as those we may lack.

4. **Support from Others:** The support and encouragement we receive from those with a vested interest in our success.

5. **Concerted Effort:** The amount of infrastructure and planning necessary to be successful—the level of investment of all our resources.

Eliminate (what doesn't matter)

Once we know what matters—what our 'X' is—then it's time to jettison everything that *doesn't* matter. I know what you're thinking, that it's not that simple. You have lots of responsibilities. You can't simply wake up one morning and say you're not going to do something anymore. Slow down. We'll cross that bridge soon enough. But remember, it was our inattention to the economics of performing with intent that got us here in the first place. The idea that we can be everything to everybody isn't sustainable, so hard decisions need to be made. This section will help us do exactly that. Specifically, it will help us:

- **Recognize:** Learn to recognize the psychological mechanisms that cause us to hang on to the worthless at the expense of the valuable.

- **Resign:** Understand that for us to be successful we're going to have to make some hard choices.

- **Take Charge:** Take control of the wheel and tell those who would try to usurp our authority to take a hike.

- **Eliminate and Prioritize:** Clean up our lives so we're focused on the right things and for the right reasons.

Plan (what matters)

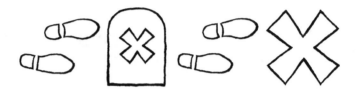

With our 'X' clearly defined and the clutter removed from the map, we can now start planning our journey to what matters. Like a seafarer studying his charts with a magnifying glass, the course becomes clear when we look closely at where we want to go and how we can get there. We set our objectives and identify milestones against which we can track our progress. We inventory the resources we need to accomplish the journey and plan for potential obstacles and threats. The better we plan, the better our odds of success. Like the sea captains of old, we can better manage our journey and increase our odds of success by detailing, tracking, and measuring our progress. To do all this we'll map out our:

1. **North Star:** Why we do what we do.
2. **Path:** How we do what we do.
3. **Destination:** Where we're going in the long-term.
4. **Milestones:** Where we're going in the short-term.
5. **Steps:** What we're going to do right now to make it all happen.

Take Action (with intent)

Life's journeys are full of obstacles, both from outside and from within. Despite all our best planning, people will challenge our commitment and cause us to waver from time to time. Economies will change, problems will arise, and life circumstances will be turned on-end. Always, an easy path of least resistance will tempt us away from our goals. As though this wasn't bad enough, maybe the most difficult part of performing with intent is allowing ourselves to do exactly that—*perform*. Working with energy and passion toward something that matters can feel self-indulgent, as though we're not supposed to enjoy work this much. Taking action means developing the tools and techniques we need to forge ahead in the face of these external and internal pressures that would confound our progress. It means recognizing those things that would cause us to deviate from our path and taking measures to keep our trajectory steady and true.

BENEFITS OF FOLLOWING THE ADEPT MODEL

The goal of the ADEPT Model is to help us perform with intent. This means accomplishing a task, not only with exceptional quality, but also with deliberate purpose. The frantic employee, manager, parent, student, or entrepreneur racing about in a discombobulated state is giving quite a show of busy energy, but is lacking focus and deliberate purpose. This will make it very difficult for these people to deliver anything with meaning and quality.

Here are a few of the benefits of performing with intent:

► You'll be more effective.

► You'll produce better quality.

► You'll deliver better results.

► You'll reduce stress.

► You'll feel greater satisfaction and self-determination.

► You'll find greater meaning in life.

Sound good? I hope so. To me there's nothing more fulfilling than accomplishing something I set out to do—something that I feel is important. If, in some small way, I can help others embrace life with similar vigor then sign me up. This is why I teach; this is why I write. I truly believe our potential is limitless. All we need is a nudge in the right direction and a little shot of courage to accomplish extraordinary things. As Ralph Waldo Emerson said, "The only person you are destined to become is the person you decide to be."

In Summary

1. **You have no one to blame but yourself:** Yes, you're insanely busy, but the reasons you're busy are more within your control than you might think.

2. **The ADEPT Model can help you regain control:** The ADEPT Model is all about helping you accomplish what matters most—that which gives you the greatest meaning and purpose in life.

Your Turn

Ready to become that person—someone who lives with purpose and intent? While this book offers a clear process to achieve what's most important to you, seeing these results will require you to apply the model in your life. To help you do this I've included several questions at the end of key sections. That's when you'll actually put pen to paper (or type into whatever electronic equivalent works best for you), and plan your future success.

So now it's your turn. Here are some things to ask yourself. Be honest. What you write will be for your eyes only.

► Summarize this chapter in your own words. Write down the key points you want your future self to know and remember.

_____

_____

_____

_____

_____

_____

_____

► Make a list of all the plates you're currently spinning. Don't worry if you can't think of everything. Later you can come back and add to the list as things come to mind.

_____

_____

_____

_____

_____

_____

▶ Reflect on why you add more and more plates to your stage. Do you want to have it all? Do you like to be busy? Do you have a hard time saying *no*?

_____

_____

_____

_____

_____

_____

_____

▶ Write of a time in your life when you felt on top of the world, a time you felt fulfilled in your endeavors; you had energy for today and excitement for tomorrow, and maybe even felt a little invincible. (If that's right now, then great! You'll still want to do this exercise so you can understand it, sustain it, and replicate it.) What plates did you have spinning at that time? What made it so memorable? How did you get from there to where you are now?

_____

_____

_____

_____

_____

_____

_____

_____

► Do you have a busy yet barren life? If so, in what ways? If not, what about your life do you find fulfilling?

_____

_____

_____

_____

_____

_____

_____

_____

Trust me, the answers to these questions will come in handy later on. In fact, you'll want to keep your notebook close by as you work your way through the ADEPT Model.

So Here's a Thought...

Someone gives you a million dollars, but with one condition: you have to invest it in something that has purpose and meaning to you. None of this go-on-a-vacation or buy-a-new-car nonsense; something that improves you and those around you. What would that be? Imagine it and write about how it would change your life.

CHAPTER 3: ACCEPT
(the economics of performing with intent)

> The first lesson of economics is scarcity: there is never enough of anything to fully satisfy all those who want it. The first lesson of politics is to disregard the first lesson of economics.
>
> *– Thomas Sowell*
> *American economist, social theorist, political philosopher*

The first lesson of politics may be to disregard the first law of economics, but this failing is not particular to politicians. Our appetite for more—regardless of how much we have—seems to be insatiable. Nonetheless, for us to succeed we need to accept and embrace the three economic laws of performing with intent:

1. The ingredients to success are in finite supply.

2. While there is a finite supply of resources, the demand for these resources is infinite.

3. Your success lies in your ability to wisely and deliberately allocate your finite resources.

No doubt you already understand these laws. A lack of understanding isn't what's preventing us from being as successful as we might be otherwise. Our struggle rests with *accepting* these principles. *Accepting* these laws is the first step in the ADEPT Model.

In the field of psychology, *acceptance* is allowing, embracing, or experiencing something which in the past we attempted to ignore or avoid.[1] There are plenty of things we know and understand but don't want to accept. We understand that weight loss comes from a combination of diet and exercise, yet we keep looking for pills and celebrity secrets to help us to slim down without any of this pesky self-denial, hard work nonsense. We understand that living within our means and saving for our retirement is the smart thing to do, but we have difficulty denying ourselves the things we want today. Add to this our consumption-based economy, geared toward delivering all manner of luxuries on credit, and the idea of going without seems unnecessarily ascetic.

To be fair, we're sort of hardwired to want. Our behavior is to a great degree guided by built-in incentive systems geared toward perpetuating species. These systems both stimulate and reward us, making it easy, even pleasurable, to keep doing whatever it takes to survive.[2] Thing is, this base firmware afforded us by evolution doesn't always know when a need has been satisfied. It's only function is to guarantee the survival of the species, no matter what. Imagine this sort of exchange going on in my subconscious:

INCENTIVE SYSTEM: "You want that $8,000 watch."

ME: "What do you mean? I have a watch."

INCENTIVE SYSTEM: "Your watch is lame. It won't attract a hot sexy mate."

ME: "What are you talking about? I'm already married to a wonderful woman and have five kids. My procreation duties are over."

INCENTIVE SYSTEM: "People laugh at your $12 watch. If you buy this one they'll think you're successful and refined. You'll get jobs and promotions."

ME: "I'm a professor at a community college. I really don't think an $8,000 watch is going to make any difference."

INCENTIVE SYSTEM: "Daredevil pilots circumnavigate the globe using nothing but this watch and the stars to navigate by."

ME: "I'm not even a pilot!"

INCENTIVE SYSTEM: "But it would be cool if you were. Chicks dig pilots."

ME: "Listen, I already told you…"

INCENTIVE SYSTEM: "You're a loser. If you buy this watch you'll be a winner. Each time you feel the weight of it on your wrist or check to see the time you'll be reminded how successful you are."

ME: "…Okay, you've got a point."

Now for the record, I don't own an $8,000 watch. (But you have to admit, the Breitling Navitimer World is a pretty awesome piece of kit.)

THE THREE ECONOMIC LAWS OF PERFORMING WITH INTENT

Between 2012 and 2014 chocolate prices rose by over 60 percent. The reason for this was simple: people were eating more chocolate than the world could produce. But there's a lot to this. Dry weather in the Ivory Coast and Ghana where more than 70 percent of the world's cocoa is grown had a negative effect on production. Then there

While I am busy with little things, I am not required to do greater things.

– Saint Francis de Sales

was a nasty fungal disease known as *frosty pod* that wiped out between 30 and 40 percent of global cocoa production. Faced with such challenges, many cocoa farmers called it quits and shifted production to less volatile, more profitable crops. All the while demand continued to rise, especially in countries like China where a burgeoning middleclass was developing a taste for the confection.[1] As a result, chocolate prices skyrocketed.

Most of us are familiar with the economic principles of supply and demand. As you know—indeed, as you undoubtedly experience daily—the microeconomic law of demand states that the more we raise the price of a product or service, the lower the demand will become. It's pretty intuitive. This is the story of our precious chocolate over the last few years. Low supply and high prices have made chocolate less of a staple and more of an indulgence. Of course the opposite holds true as well: the lower the price the greater the demand.

Now (and this is important), when the price for a product or service is set below what is called the *equilibrium price*, this creates what is known as *excess demand*. Because the price is set so low, more consumers want the product or service than the producer is able to deliver. In other words, the producer has set the price so low that now he's unable to meet demand. Ideally the producer would like the supply and demand to be at *equilibrium*. This is optimal in terms of efficiency because the supply of the product or service exactly meets the demand (or pretty darn close, anyway).

We *get* this, we *know* this. So if that's the case, why then do we not *accept* this when it comes to how we allocate our own scarce resources? As we will see, time, energy, and cognitive resources are in finite supply, and yet demand for these resources is practically infinite. This seems to fly in the face of the principles of supply and demand, until we look at one fact:

We are undervaluing our time, energy, and cognitive resources.

With the price set so low, it's no wonder that demand is so high. Our job then is to raise the price of our resources and achieve equilibrium. With this in mind, let's take a look at the three laws:

1. Supply Is Finite

The ingredients to success are in finite supply. Thing is, we don't much like the idea of limitations. We take out loans, purchase on credit, and pump oil like it's going out of style. It's not that we don't understand that these are finite resources, we just don't want the fact to unduly inconvenience our lives. It's an ethical dilemma we struggle with continuously: whether to consume today or to conserve for tomorrow. Sometimes we strike a good balance; other times not so much. Nevertheless, success and sustainability requires us to take a good hard look at the resources we bring to bear and come to terms with their unforgiving finite nature.

Cognitive Resources

Cognitive resources are what allow us to process information, think clearly, and respond to those around us in a thoughtful, deliberate, and considered manner. Think of them as good ol' brain power. They allow us to make informed decisions and navagate the course of the day. They also, quite frankly, help us keep it together then everything is falling to pieces. Self-control, willpower, focus, and concentration all draw on our pool of cognitive resources, as does our ability to make good decisions and solve problems.

Like everything else we bring to the party, our cognitive resources are easily, quickly, and inevitably depleted. As the day wears on we're less able to focus on the work at hand, exercise restraint, or make good decisions. It's the proverbial father coming home and kicking the dog. All day he's had to deal with the chaos of work and restrain himself from lashing out. Now, at the end of the day, his cognitive resources are depleted. He's tired and grumpy, quick with harsh words, and generally unpleasant to be around. Or how about the mother who has put in a hard day's work and is coming home late, dead tired, wanting nothing more than a half hour to herself to replenish her soul? And there, waiting at the door, are her kids and husband, asking what's for dinner. Heaven save this family from the lashing they're about to receive! The day has exhausted this woman's cognitive resources, and no matter how much she may love her family, she has nothing left to muster. This father and mother aren't beasts or uncaring parents; they're all of us, trying to meter out our limited cognitive resources throughout the day, and falling short in the process.

A study conducted by Baba Shiv of the University of Iowa and Alexander Fedorikhin at Washington State University illustrates this point. The researchers divided the participants into two groups. One group was asked to memorize a two-digit number. Meanwhile the second group was asked to memorize a seven-digit number. Next the participants were directed to a room down the hall. Waiting for them was a choice of two snacks: some fruit salad or a piece of chocolate cake. What the researchers found was the participants who were asked to memorize a seven-digit number were almost twice as likely to choose the cake as those who had to memorize the two-digit number. It turns out that the participants who had to memorize the longer number had a greater "cognitive load" placed upon them. This in turn reduced their ability to make a better snack decision and resist the cake. To put it another way, their willpower had been diminished by the cognitive task of remembering a number.[1] The same thing happens to us, of course. As the day wears on and uses up our cognitive resources we're less able to reason, problem solve, or make good decisions. Have you ever binge-eaten at the end of the day? Well there you go.

Energy

The story of the first marathon goes something like this: in 546 BCE the Persian Empire extended from Asia to Egypt to what's now Turkey. Poor little Greece, on the other hand, consisted of a smattering of independent city-states. Of these city-states, Athens was the largest and most prosperous.

Over the years the Persian Empire expanded to the Mediterranean Sea, conquering a handful of Greek settlements along the way. For a while the occasional revolt kept the Persians occupied, but by 490 BCE the empire had things well enough in hand and was poised to expand its territory in to Europe. Confident in their prowess, they landed a large force right outside of Athens on the plains of Marathon and prepared to attack.

Athens was in trouble, and they knew it. Vastly outnumbered, they desperately needed the help of Sparta and its military machine. So the Athenian generals sent a renowned runner named Phidippides to Sparta, a journey of something like 145 miles over jagged mountains and rugged trails. It took him about 36 hours but eventually Phidippides arrived and made his plea. The Spartans agreed to help, but not until the next full moon. With this less-than-perfect news Phidippides ran back to join his troops and with them marched into battle on the plains of Marathon. The Athenian army was outnumbered four to one but they launched an offensive that caught the Persian's by surprise. By the time the dust settled 6,400 Persian bodies lay dead on the field. By contrast, less than 200 Athenians had been lost.

Smarting from their defeat, the Persian army fled to the sea and headed south to Athens. The idea was to get to the city before the Athenian army could reassemble and get back to defend their homes. Again the generals called upon Phidippides and ordered him to run to Athens, 26 miles away, and tell the city of their victory but also of the approaching Persian ships. Despite his extreme fatigue, having run somewhere in the neighborhood of 300 miles and battled the Persians all morning, Phidippides once again obeyed

> *"Coaches and bosses ask for 110 percent. Talk about our distain for the reality of limited resources!"*

and set off for Athens. A few hours later he stood before his city and said, "Hail, we are the winners," then dropped dead from exhaustion. Soon after, Sparta and the other Greek city-states came to the aid of Athens and pushed back the Persian army.

The moral of the story? Energy is not limitless. Whenever I hear somebody say they want someone to give 100 percent, I think to myself, "When a horse gives 100 percent it dies." But people don't ask for 100 percent. Coaches and bosses ask for 110 percent. Talk about our distain for the reality of limited resources!

Time

There are 60 seconds in a minute, 60 minutes in an hour, 24 hours in a day, and 365 days in a year. These figures are pretty darn absolute. (Well, okay. There are in fact 365 days, 5 hours, 48 minutes, and 46 seconds in a year, hence the occasional leap year, but you get my point.) At every moment of every day we have to make decisions on how best to use our time. If we do this well then we weigh the demands of work, home, personal time, and other obligations, prioritize these demands, then execute that plan. Unfortunately this isn't often what we do. Most the time it seems the squeaky wheel gets the grease. Whatever demand is screaming the loudest gets our time. And in today's market economy, what screams loudest is often the job.

Today we're spending more time working, much of it from home after regular business hours.[2] We eat lunch at our desks, stay late, take work home over the weekends, and answer email while sitting on the sidelines at our kids' soccer games. (At this very moment, as I edit this chapter, I'm attending my daughter's drill team competition. Don't worry, her team isn't up yet.) Over the last few decades Americans have overtaken the rest of the industrialized world when it comes to time spent working. Americans take less vacation, work longer days, and retire later in life.[3] Juliet Schor, author of the best-selling book, *The Overworked American*, found that in 1990 Americans worked on average nearly one month more per year than they had in 1970. Her findings met with some controversy, but the anecdotal evidence for most American workers would seem to support Schor's findings.[4]

Not that every moment of every day is going to the workplace. Housework sees more than two hours a day.[5] Then on top of that, nearly everyone ages 15 and over engages in somewhere between five and six hours a day in some sort of leisure activity. Of this time, close to half is dedicated to watching TV.[6] Then there's caring for children and other loved ones, participating in community and religious activities, personal development, and so forth. Everyone wants on our calendars—including us.

All this means we're trying to fit more and more activities in what is, in the end, a finite and highly inflexible resource. We've all wished there were more hours in the day, but there aren't, so we look for ways to maximize what time we do have. We do all kinds of things to try and slow the hands of time, but time marches on nonetheless. There are strategies we can employ to squeeze more productivity out of each hour, and later we'll discuss these in detail. However, many come at a cost in terms of energy and cognitive performance.

A Quick Note Aboute Buying Time

We often look for ways to get more hours out of the day so we can be more productive. The problem is there's no such thing as a free lunch; everything comes at a price. For example, it may feel like the least productive time of our day is that spent sleeping, so we stay up late or get up early. We figure if we can squeeze a few more hours out of the day then we'll come out ahead. However, trading sleep for time comes at a cost to our cognitive resources. We can only work so long before our ability to make good decisions and perform at a high level diminishes. By starting the day tired we've already put ourselves into a cognitive deficit.

Another way we try to artificially create more time is by working insane hours. We may be able to pull this off now and again, but it's not sustainable. The body and mind need rest if they're going to replenish their energy stores. In this way we can convert one limited resource (energy) into another (time), but only to a point.

All this is very similar to the first law of thermodynamics: energy cannot be created or destroyed; it can only be converted from one state to another. Likewise, we cannot create more of any one resource; we can only convert one resource into another. Need more time? It will cost you energy and cognitive resources. This means when it comes to the ingredients necessary for success, they're precious. We should therefore treat them as such.

2. Demand Is Infinite

While there's a finite supply of resources, the demand for these resources is infinite. There's no end to those who want a piece of us. As we discussed earlier, employers, clients, and customers are always demanding more. Families as well want our evenings and weekends, our attendance at games and recitals.

Most of these demands we filter out, almost without realizing a request for our attention has even been made. We see yet don't see billboards on the highway, store signs, ads on TV, on social media, even on our phone apps. Sure, now and again they slip into our conscious view, but the vast majority are efficiently filtered out. If they weren't, we'd go insane. We apply these same filters to other demands on our attention. As it's said, the squeaky wheel gets the grease. We filter out all but the most immediate and instant demands on our attention. The problem is, *immediate and insistent* may not always equal *important*.

When we look at all of the demands placed upon our limited resources, it's a good idea to categorize them so we can better understand where we're investing our time and why. Here are some ways we might consider prioritizing our tasks:

Physiological Needs

Our physiological needs are those things our bodies require to function, things like sleep, nutrients, and relaxation. Sure, we can try to minimize the time investment we make in these seemingly mundane needs, but that comes at a cost. For instance, we may choose to sleep less or eat our lunches at our desks. This may seem like a good trade—less time spent on "low return" physiological needs and more time spent producing—but the costs can exceed the benefits. Sleep deprivation, even a little, can negatively affect our ability to be productive.

Lack of sleep impairs our decision-making processes and stifles creativity.[1] Our emotions can also be affected, making us more likely to become short tempered and experience mood swings. Overall the lack of sleep diminishes our cognitive functions.[2]

But what about eating lunch at our desks? Surely that's a productive use of time otherwise spent on meeting base physiological needs. In 2012 only one-in-five American office employees took a lunch break away from their desks, so clearly the trend has taken hold.[3] However, strange as it may sound, this practice introduces a host of health and productivity risks. Prolonged sedentary time has been associated with negative health outcomes, even among those who are physically active away from work.[4] Forgoing breaks also has ramifications when it comes to our cognitive resources. A meal away from the office with others can be relaxing and put our frazzled nerves on hold for a while.[5] In fact, the very act of socializing during lunch can have a positive effect on our ability to thrive. Failure to take breaks can drain our ability to regulate emotions throughout a working day. As we've discussed, each time we engage in some sort of self-control our psychological resources become depleted. Taking a time-out breaks up the day and allows our self-control a chance to take a breather.[6] It's like going on a long run: break it up with a series of short walks and you can go farther than if you tried to run the entire distance. Furthermore, what we do in those short breaks can make a difference as well. Research has suggests that taking a break and visiting green spaces can have a restorative effect, improving attention fatigue and quickening stress recovery.[7]

No matter how we cut it, our physiological needs must be met. Ignore them and they'll take it out of us, one way or the other.

Obligations

Obligations are those duties which we are morally, ethically, or legally bound to perform. There are any number of obligations we must meet in the course of our daily lives. As parents we're obligated to provide our children with a safe nurturing home environment. We're obligated to provide them with an education. Failure to provide these things is considered a breach of a moral, ethical, and legal contract which society has chosen to place on the role of parenthood. As homeowners we're obligated to keep our yards nice and tidy in accordance with city ordinances. As citizens we're obligated to vote and pay taxes. In the case of voting, we're not legally required to cast our ballot, but there is nonetheless an implied obligation for all citizens to participate in the democratic process. The lack of a coercive element or a legal consequence does not change the fact it's an obligation. Whether we do these things or not is another issue, but failing to meet an obligation does not mean it doesn't exist.

We're not going to get out of meeting our obligations (nor should you want to). However, we can make sure they get no more than the appropriate allocation of our resources, depending on what matters most.

Commitments

Commitments are those activities, causes, or projects to which we have voluntarily chosen to dedicate ourselves. Unlike our obligations, commitments are not attached to any social or moral contract. This isn't to say they aren't important. Some might be extremely important, but *extremely important* is not the same as *do it or remove yourself from civil society*. We need to understand this distinction because when it comes time to prioritize our goals and eliminate those that don't matter it won't do to blithely eliminate an obligation so we can spend more time on a commitment. Literature and song are replete with stories of fathers on their deathbed, wishing they'd spent more time with their children and less in the boardroom. These people neglected their obligations as fathers in favor of their commitments as employees. It wasn't until it was too late that they realized the existential costs of their decisions.

Examples of commitments that often get confused with obligations are careers, vocations, board positions, coaching responsibilities, club memberships, or business ventures. Even some leisure activities can begin to feel like obligations. A friend of mine owns a timeshare. Since he's making payments on this thing month after month, year after year, the idea of *not* using the timeshare becomes very difficult to swallow. These people run the risk of becoming slaves to their investment, obediently making the obligatory pilgrimage each year, sometimes with little to no joy involved. Now and again he tries to give away a week here and there to family. It's a generous offer, but I can't help the feeling that it's tinged with a bit of, "Please, free me from this commitment!"

Avocations

Avocations are our hobbies and minor occupations. Working on cars, gardening, painting, participating in sports, going to the gym, playing an instrument, and camping are all examples of avocations. They are separate from our careers or vocations in that they are meant to channel our passions and interests in a way that allow us to self-actualize.

Just as commitments sometimes take on the weight of obligations, avocations can start to smell and taste like commitments. Someone who plays in a band on the weekend or cycles with a group of friends in the evening may feel like he's committed to the activity, but in truth it's a hobby. This isn't to say that an avocation can't push out a commitment to make space. It all depends on what matters most—what that person's 'X' may be at that moment. But it's still important to make the differentiation to keep our chosen activities in perspective. Many like to put on disguises to try and move up the priority ladder. Everthing wants to be important.

Recreations

Recreations are those things we do to decompress, empty our brains, and just plain relax. This can include watching TV, going to a movie, reading a book, taking a drive in the canyon, playing a video game, and so forth. Sometimes these things are called "timewasters," but I wouldn't be so hasty. We can't be "on" all the time. We need to power down now and again. In fact, engaging in relaxing recreational activities such as watching TV, listening to music, or doing puzzles can reduce stress and be healthful for us.[8] The problem arises when we power down too long or too often. I've seen many cases where someone's commitments or even obligations suffered because the person (Ah heck, who am I kidding? Me!) dedicated too much time to distractions. As we saw earlier, nearly everyone spends somewhere between five and six hours a day in some sort of leisure activity, and close to half of this time is spent watching TV.[9] That comes out to something close to three hours of television a day. Today, with dozens of networks producing shows, DVRs in practically every home, and all kinds of on-demand and streaming services available, watching TV is easier than ever. Think about it: three hours accounts for almost 20 percent of our waking day. If obligations and commitments hang in the balance, recreations can be problematic.

Know the Difference

It's easy to unconsciously move our activities up and down this continuum as we try to prioritize our finite resources. By taking stock of our obligations, commitments, avocations, and recreations we can be more deliberate in assigning resources to our activities. This is good because if we don't prioritize our time, someone else will. When they do, we can be assured

> *"If we don't prioritize our time, someone else will."*

they'll state their requests in the strongest possible terms. Consider the opening clause, "I need you to…" Need? Really? What, after all, constitutes a need? Our family has a running joke: whenever one of us really, really wants something that we know is an extravagance we playfully sing out, "I neeeeeed…" The truth is we'd be surprised how little we actually need.

3. Resources Must Be Allocated Wisely

Our success lies in our ability to wisely and deliberately allocate our finite resources. Imagine there's a coin that represents our time, energy, and cognitive resources. Now let's say we have 100 of these coins, each representing one percent of our daily allotment of resources. In walks a thousand people, each asking us for our coins. Some represent physiological needs and obligations, others represent commitments, avocations, and recreations. Each offers us something in exchange for a few of our coins, something that has a given level of value to us. However, there's no way we can afford everything offered with the mere handful of coins we have. But this doesn't dissuade all those in the room from hustling us for our resources. They press forward, making the hard sell. All are insistent, some even coercive. Each tells us that in paying them our coins we'll be happier and more fulfilled than we would be otherwise. In fact, each person accosting us would just assume we give him the majority of our coins. It's as though each is oblivious to the others in the room, demanding our coins right alongside them. Everyone seems to be in it for themselves, each saying that what they are offering is the most important, most valuable, most desirable thing we could ever hope to have. At the end of the day though our options are limited, so we evaluate our choices, prioritize our needs and wants, then make our decisions.

This is the world we face every day, and each day we have to decide how best to allocate our precious coins. When we look at it this way it may be easier to see how precious and valuable our time, energy, and cognitive resources are—how carefully we should distribute these treasures. With this in mind, there are some important points to consider:

You Are Less Effective When You Spread Out Your Attention

Remember when as kids we lit leaves on fire with a magnifying glass? Wasn't that awesome?! There we were, basking safely in the diffused rays of the sun, but focus those same ways on a single point and presto! Instant death ray! (Don't tell me if you killed ants. I did that once and felt awful afterwards.) Using our limited resources is no different. A modicum of our time and mindshare is not the same as our full and undivided attention. It's tempting to believe we're making a difference in a lot of areas by taking on multiple projects and causes, but in fact we may be hurting these efforts more than helping them. For example, companies with board members who hold three or more directorships exhibit lower market-to-book ratios and weaker profitability. Simply put, the board members' attention is too divided to provide quality governance to the company.[1] Another example can be found in my vast catalogue of unfinished novels. I have easily six or seven books in various stages of completion, yet none are anywhere near what one might consider "done." In the interest of full disclosure, I'm easily distracted by shiny objects, especially when it comes to book ideas. I spend all kinds of time planning and outlining these ideas, even writing something like a first draft, but then somehow I lose steam and start looking for my next idea. This is no way to be successful as a writer, or in any other endeavor for that matter. It's like trying to bore a hole into a lead wall with a flashlight rather than a laser. If our goal is to perform with intent then we need to fully focus on the task.

You Can't Go into Debt

It's a simple principle: don't spend more than you make. But as we've already shown, living within our means is easier said than done. This is true financially, and no less so for our lives. However, if we're going to achieve what really matters, living within our means is exactly what we need to do.

In his book, *The Total Money Makeover*, author Dave Ramsey offers this motto for his system: "If you will live like no one else, later you can live like no one else."[2] The idea is if we're willing to make the hard choices today and jealously guard our money, allocating it only to where it can have the most impact, then we'll be able to accomplish what few others have and reap significant rewards in the future. This principle is no less applicable when it comes to how we invest our time, energy, and cognitive resources.

No One Is Going to Guard Your Resources for You

It's easy to become overwhelmed as teams of people and interests mob us with demands for our time. We can even grow to resent them, feeling put upon by their incessant requests. The truth though is they're not to blame for the pressure we feel; we are. They have no idea what's on our plate, all the obligations, commitments, avocations, and recreations we've signed ourselves up for. Only we have the big picture in mind when it comes to our own lives. This means it's our job to set the limits and prioritize. Resenting bosses, teachers, families, or other interests for loading on the pressure is tantamount to abdicating our responsibilities and blaming others for our inability to set boundaries.

You're Only as Free to Succeed as Your Resources Allow

This is what this book is all about: how to identify what matters most, eliminate everything else, and achieve great things. We're fond of saying that we're free to do whatever we want. The truth is we're free do whatever *our resources allow*. I may be free to go to Paris, but if I lack the resources to do so then I'm no freer to go to Paris than someone locked in a jail cell. Our lack of resources constrain us—constrain us to doing only that which really and truly matters. (And as much as I would love to go to Paris, it's not a priority at this time.) What we need to do therefore is figure out what really matters and focus our efforts there. Soon, that's exactly what we'll be doing.

In Summary

1. **Time, energy, and cognitive resources are limited:** There's only so much of these resources available to you each day.

2. **Resources can't be created:** These limited resources can't be created; they can only be converted (but even this comes at a cost).

3. **There's no end to the demand for your resources:** Your resources may be in limited supply, but the demand for these resources is infinite.

4. **It's your responsibility to set boundaries:** No one can see the big picture of your life like you can, so it's your job to prioritize your activities.

5. **Not all demands are created equal:** There's an inherent hierarchy to the demands placed upon you.

6. **You're successful when you intelligently allocate your finite resources:** It's up to you to decide where to invest your limited resources. This is where your ability to accomplish great things rests.

7. **You're less effective when you spread out your resources:** By focusing the rays of the sun on a single spot you can wield greater power than if the light is diffused.

8. **You can't go into debt:** You can't borrow time, energy, or cognitive resources from tomorrow to use today. In all three cases you get a daily allocation; no more.

9. **Restraint brings freedom to succeed:** It may sound like an oxymoron, but the more you deny yourself things that needlessly tax your limited resources, the more you'll have to accomplish incredible things.

Your Turn

As we discussed, nothing in this chapter is necessarily new; what it may be however is conveniently disregarded. It's time to change this and make your limited resources work for you, rather than the other way around. With this in mind, get out your notebook, find a quiet place, and review your thoughts from chapter one. Add freely to your notes with these questions as your guide:

▶ How well do you manage your time?

_____

_____

_____

_____

_____

_____

_____

_____

▶ Do you feel in charge of your resources—your time, energy, and cognitive resources—or do you feel beholden to other masters?

_____

_____

_____

_____

_____

_____

_____

_____

▶ What's the "price" you've set for your time, energy, and cognitive resources? The price isn't likely to be in dollars and cents, so what's the currency? Why's the price set where it is? Is it the right price?

_____

_____

_____

_____

_____

_____

_____

▶ Refer to your list of spinning plates and place them in their categories: Physiological Needs, Obligations, Commitments, Avocations, and Recreations. This isn't a test; there are no right or wrong answers. It's a simple analysis to help you understand where you spend your limited resources. When you look at the results, does the distribution of your time and effort makes sense, or is it skewed?

_____

_____

_____

_____

_____

_____

_____

▶ Have you ever thought about all you could accomplish if only you had
   more time? What are some of those things you dream about doing?

_____

_____

_____

_____

_____

_____

_____

_____

Painful? A little uncomfortable? Don't worry; this is the first step in taking
control of your life and deciding how best to use your time and talents. At
this early stage the exercises may be uncomfortable, but trust me, they'll soon
become energizing and empowering!

So Here's a Thought...

Have you ever looked back at all the foolish purchases you've made over the years and imagined what you could do with all that money today had you not wasted it? What about your time? What if you could have all your wasted time given back to you in one lump sum, what would you do with it?

CHAPTER 4: DISCOVER
(what really matters)

There are two great days in a person's life—the day we are born and the day we discover why.

– William Barclay

Scottish author, presenter, professor at the University of Glasgow

Now that we've accepted that we need to wisely allocate our resources to perform with intent, the next step is to determine where to apply these resources for greatest effect. This means figuring out what matters to us the most—or as Simon Sinek might call it—figuring out our *why*. It's by understanding our *why* that we'll be able to find joy in what we do and inspire others to support us.[1] Understanding and pursing our *why*—that which matters most to us and gives us purpose and meaning—allows us to tap into our intrinsic motivation. (More on this later.) Indeed, we won't only be motivated to succeed; we'll be *inspired* to do so. Remember the thousands of salesmen, all wanting our time, energy, and cognitive resource coins? These people all operate from the same playbook, which is telling us that what they have is the most important thing on the planet and that we need to allocate at least some of our coins to buying what they're selling. When we know what matters and what doesn't, the sirens singing us to our deaths in the cliffs lose their power to steer us off course.

Understanding what's important can also help us rally the support of those around us. In the movie *Selma* there's a scene in which Dr. Martin Luther King, Jr. is trying to make his case to President Lyndon B. Johnson. The president is sympathetic to King's cause, but in response he has to tell the activist, "You got one issue; I got a hundred and one."[2] We can all relate to the president's plea for patience and understanding. However, there's also no disputing the righteousness of Dr. King's cause or the need for swift and decisive leadership from the highest office in the land. Dr. King understood what was most important, and armed with a righteous *why*, he was able to win the president over to his cause.

Finally, discovering our purpose enables us to see new meaning in the many facets of our lives. Day-to-day tasks that in the past may have felt tedious or mundane take on new meaning and importance. It's sort of like when I was living in Japan and trying to improve my language skills. Back then I started each morning by choosing five new words to add it to my working vocabulary. Then as I would go about my day I would try to work these words into the conversation. The practice worked fine, but I noticed something interesting. It seemed like everywhere I went I heard these words all over the place. It was as though everyone in Japan had chosen these same words to use over and over for my benefit. Obviously this wasn't the case, so what was happening? As it turns out, these words were all around me every day; I just didn't hear them because I wasn't focusing on them. Likewise, things that give us meaning are woven all throughout our lives. By focusing on them we can see them everywhere, thereby finding new meaning in old tasks. Understanding what gives us purpose is like shining an ultraviolet light on our lives. As if by magic every meaningful thing that was once hidden now glows forth in marvelous living detail.

As we'll see, it's hard to overstate the power of purpose. When you forget to eat and shower for days on end because you're working on something that excites you, then you start to recognize the awesome power of purpose. Chances are you know this, but then you also know that finding your purpose is a tricky thing. Some of us know what we want to do from an early age (lucky jerks), but most of us wander through life, going here, going there, letting a series of random events navigate our lives. This isn't *Discovering* what gives us purpose; this is letting fate decide our lot in life.

Discovering what's important to us is the next step of the ADEPT Model. In the end, no one can decide what's meaningful to you but you. So let's figure out what that is; let's uncover our 'X.'

YOU CREATE YOUR OWN PURPOSE AND MEANING

No one can decide what gives you purpose and meaning but you. No one. Just you. What's more, it can be anything—*anything*—you like. It's the greatest superpower possessed of humanity, and it's yours to command as you will. Let me show you what I mean by introducing you to Sisyphus, Viktor Farnkl, and Dennis.

> **Your time is limited, so don't waste it living someone else's life.**
>
> – *Steve Jobs*

The Greek Antihero Sisyphus

As far as scoundrels went, Sisyphus was a real piece of work. Abundantly clever and deceitful, the Greek antihero used his considerable gifts to torment those around him. One moment he would welcome travelers into his home; the next he would murder them and toss their bodies out to be devoured by beasts. Crafty and avaricious, he seduced his niece then stole his brother's throne. An equal opportunity tormentor, he brought no end of grief to the gods of Olympus as well. On a lark he decided to spread secrets of Zeus' sexual exploits all about town. Well as it turns out, the king of the gods wasn't amused so he commanded Hades to personally go up with a pair of handcuffs and collect Sisyphus himself. But our friend still had a few tricks up his tunic. Feigning interest in the curious handcuffs, the wily Sisyphus asked Hades to demonstrate how the things worked, which the god of the underworld did—on himself. Before he knew it Hades was locked in a closet while all around world the cycle of life and death went all catawampus. Yep, he was a real rapscallion.

Eventually things caught up with Sisyphus. He was finally dragged down to the underworld where the gods had devised a beautifully ingenious fate worthy of Sisyphus' wit. As punishment, Sisyphus was damned to an eternity of rolling a boulder up a giant hill, only to have the immense stone slip away mere inches from the top and roll back down to the valley below. Over and over, without end, Sisyphus would follow the boulder down to the bottom, set his shoulder against the great rock, and start the process all over again. It's scarcely possible to think of a more diabolical fate; a task so repetitive and endless, so taxing, and yet so completely utterly meaningless, one wonders how anything could be worse.

His punishment was eternal, so we can today imagine Sisyphus down there still, endlessly pushing on his well-worn stone. As far as the world is concerned Sisyphus' purpose and meaning has been defined by his punishment: to roll the stone to the top of the hill. His fate is what it is. The gods have decreed it, and there's no use fighting the gods. Indeed, if his desire is to roll the stone to the top of the hill and then stop, he will be forever miserable.

If he's ever going to be at peace with his endless and meaningless task then something has to change, and since he can't beat the gods, this means changing his objective. By doing this he can steal the power away from the gods and take it for himself. No longer will the gods decide his misery based on the presumed objective of rolling the stone up the hill. Sisyphus can take control of his own purpose by taking the objective away from the gods and owning it himself!

What might this look like? Maybe he decides this time he's going to see if he can take a total of 1,000 steps on his way up the hill before the rock rolls back down. Then he'll see if he can do it in exactly 999, and so forth. Later he might see if once the rock starts rolling down he can beat it to the bottom. After that he might compose a song on the way up, then for kicks sing it backwards on the way back down. It really doesn't matter what objectives or purpose he sets for himself, so long as they are his own. That way success is always a possibility, and where there's the possibility of success there's purpose. Sure, the

It's a little known historical fact that Sisyphus was a massive B-52s fan.

gods might insist success looks like the rock making it all the way up the hill, but that's impossible and therefore should be discarded as an objective. Rather than banging his head against a wall for all eternity (or a stone, as the case may be), trying to force success where success is not attainable, Sisyphus needs to decide what success looks like for himself and go after that. He's still doing what the gods commanded, but not for the purpose they ordered. As a result he robs them of their punishment, and consequently their power. Sisyphus is not refusing to roll the stone up the hill; he's just refusing to do it for the reasons dictated by the gods. He's doing it for his own purposes.

In his book, *The Myth of Sisyphus*, the existentialist Albert Camus equates the plight our antihero with that of the average employee, ceaselessly toiling away at some mundane and seemingly absurd task. "The workman of today works every day in his life at the same tasks, and this fate is no less absurd. But it is tragic only at the rare moments when it becomes conscious."[1] While the task may seem meaningless and absurd, this doesn't have to be the case. We can decide the meaning. We can decide whether we find fulfillment in the task. As Camus says, "One must imagine Sisyphus happy."

Viktor Frankl and the Nazis

During WWII Viktor Frankl lived the nightmare that was the Nazi concentration camp system. He was first deported to a ghetto in Theresienstadt, then taken to Auschwitz, Kaufering, and Türkheim. In these notorious concentration camps Frankl endured all the horrors we've come to associate with the holocaust: starvation, beatings, humiliation, sickness, and all manner of cruelty we can scarcely imagine. Yet all throughout Frankl found purpose and meaning—meaning that ultimately saved his life.

In his book, *Man's Search for Meaning*, Frankl talks about the absolute need mankind has for meaning, explaining that purpose must be found in every moment and in every action we take, especially when others seek to rob us of our meaning and replace it with their own torturous purposes. Just as in the gods had imposed an impossible purpose on Sisyphus as an eternal punishment, the Nazis tried to strip away all vestiges of humanity from Frankl, and with that his meaning.[2] This left Frankl with three choices: allow his captors to decide his worth, which would likely cause him to wither away and die from despair; fight the guards and attempt to escape, probably resulting in his death; or live in rebellion to the false conditions and do all that was asked of him, but for his own reasons—thereby establishing his own meaning. (More about false conditions later.) He selected the third option, choosing to live for the memory of his family, for his research, and for the manuscript that had been stolen from him. In choosing to live for these reasons Frankl survived and went on to accomplish many great and wonderful things.

Dennis and King Arthur

In the movie *Monty Python and the Holy Grail*, King Arthur comes across a couple of peasants toiling in the mud. He calls out to one of them, presuming the person to be an old woman, only to find the peasant is actually a 37-year old man named Dennis. Arthur apologizes for the misunderstanding but Dennis is not satisfied. "What I object to is you automatically treat me like an inferior," Dennis says.[3] "Well I am king..." This is Arthur's attempt to return order to a situation which, by his reckoning, has become completely absurd and unacceptable. After all, who ever heard of a peasant talking back to the king? For the life of him he can't fathom why a serf would be treating his king with such disrespect. The idea is so inconceivable that Arthur's only reasonable conclusion is that the man must simply not know who Arthur is. But what he doesn't realize is that Dennis and his companion have their own view of hierarchy. To them the idea of strange women lying in ponds distributing swords as a basis of government is the most absurd concept of all. "King of the who?" asks Dennis' companion. King Arthur tells her that he is king of the Britons, that we are all Britons, and that therefore he is their king. Again, bringing logical order to chaos. "I didn't know we had a king," the woman says. "I thought we were an autonomous collective." Whether toiling as serfs under the fist of a merciless lord or working as an autonomous collective, the nature of the work doesn't change. What changes is the *reason* they're working. Dennis and the woman are not rebelling directly against Arthur, Briton, or the monarchy system of government. They're not organizing an underground conspiracy bent on toppling the king from his throne. What they *are* doing is living in rebellion to the idea that they should view themselves as inferior peasants and serfs, nothing more than disposable humanity, good only for enriching their feudal lords. Of course this doesn't change what's required of them. They're still toiling in the filth, collecting sod or whatever it is that they're doing in the muck, but they're not doing it because the lord has decreed it; they're doing it for their own reasons.

WHY MEANING IS SO IMPORTANT

Meaning is at the core of the human condition. It allows us to make sense of the senseless, to understand that which cannot be understood, and to chart a path into an unknowable future. It gives us a firm sense of purpose, essential for optimal human development and joy.[1] As psychologist and Harvard Pd.D. Jerome Bruner puts it, without meaning, "We would be lost in murk of chaotic experience and probably would not have survived as a species in any case."[2] For Frankl, nothing is more important to our psychological well-being than having a sense of meaning. Without it we lose our mooring. According to Frankl, psychological harm can occur when a person's search for meaning is in some way blocked or frustrated.[3] Based on these observations, Frankl developed a psychology theory called *logotherapy*. The basic tenets of logotherapy say the primary motivational force in life is to find purpose and meaning in all around us. It says:

► Meaning can be found in all circumstances, even the most horrendous.

► Our main motivation in all we do is to find meaning in life.

► We are free to find meaning in whatever we do or experience, even if all this means is assigning meaning to situations of unchangeable suffering.[4]

The key to achieving positive life purpose and meaning, Frankl teaches, is found in strong religious beliefs, membership in groups, dedication to a cause, life values, and clear goals.[5] Understanding our values, identifying those causes that are important to us, and setting clear goals is what the ADEPT Model is all about.

What Will Be Your Story?

This is the great lesson we can take away from Dennis, Frankl, and Sisyphus: that no one—not kings, not the Nazis, not even the gods—can decide our purpose and meaning. That awesome power is ours alone to wield!

So, what do you plan to do with this incredible power you possess?

What do you say we find out?

In Summary

1. **Meaning matters:** A sense of purpose and meaning is vital to living a happy and fulfilled life.

2. **You alone decide your meaning:** The world is full of would-be masters who will try to tell you your purpose, but they have no power but that which you give them. You alone can decide your propose.

Your Turn

Sisyphus, Frankl, and Dennis are great as far as abstract examples are concerned, but abstractions can only take us so far. Let's see if we can move this important principle from the conceptual into the read-and-now:

▶ Have you ever experienced a time when, like Sisyphus, Frankl, and Dennis, you took control and decided your own why—a time when you did what was expected of you but for your own reasons? If so, how did that make you feel? If not, how do you imagine you might feel?

_____

_____

_____

_____

_____

_____

_____

_____

▶ Who do you know that has done as Sisyphus, Frankl, and Dennis—people who did what needed to be done but for their own reasons? Do you know anyone who did what was required of them but marched to the beat of their own drummer?

_____

_____

_____

_____

_____

_____

_____

▶ Think about some of the responsibilities you face every day but don't look
   forward to. What are some ways you can reframe your approach such that
   the task might be more rewarding?

_____

_____

_____

_____

_____

_____

_____

Soon none of this will be conceptual. By the end of the ADEPT Model you'll be
brining energy and passion to most every facet of your life.

THE FIVE STEPS TO DISTILLING PRIORITIES

Many of us have busy hectic lives, full of all manner of responsibilities and obligations. Each of these commitments demands our time and attention. Sometimes these demands can be so relentless it becomes difficult to know where to invest our resources and where to push back. One way we can do this is by running our lives through something like a filter.

When I was a kid my father liked to take my brother and me camping. One day in the campground I saw a water faucet with a sign above it saying *Potable*. I asked my father about the sign and he told me it meant the water was drinkable. I wondered, if that was the case, why didn't the sign just say *Drinkable*? My childhood mind rationalized that it meant we could use the water in *pots* when cooking. I had no idea the Latin for *drinkable* was *potabilis*.[1] (Who knew you needed a degree in Latin to identify safe drinking water in a campground?)

Water goes through a variety of filtration steps before it's considered safe to drink. Some of these steps involve introducing bacteria that eat up all the nasty gross organic matter. Others use coagulation and sedimentation. Still other steps employ physical filters that strain out contaminates. Though each of these steps call on different processes, they all work together to produce safe drinking water. Similarly, we can run our lives through a series of filters to will help us distill our activities down to what is most essential.

1. Guiding Principles

A river takes the path of least resistance. Never once does it say, "Gee, I wonder which direction I should flow today." Its path is decided by the topology. Yet no one would ever call a river powerless. Water is the author of our planet. Ironically, while topology directs the river, the river creates the topology. So in a way, the river does control its path, but not by reassessing its direction every minute of every day. It does it by setting boundaries and letting those boundaries guide its direction for centuries to come.

We can control our own topology by setting guiding principles—principles that direct our behavior with little to no thought on our part. Guiding principles are values that form our attitudes and influence our decisions. For example, I value punctuality. My attitude is this: when someone is late, that person is telling me his time is more important than mine, that whatever I might have on my plate, it's nowhere near as important as what he was doing, so it's okay to make me to wait. Now don't get me wrong. I know not everyone who's running late has such cavalier and inconsiderate disregard for the time of others, but my guiding principle holds fast nonetheless. As a result of this value I'm always at least ten minute early to anything I attend—sometimes much earlier. For me it's not even negotiable. I will plan my entire day around my need to be early. Hence the power of guiding principles.

The reason guiding principles are so valuable is because they essentially serve as default settings for many of our decisions. They're the principles or precepts that guide us in all we do, regardless of our changing environment. Remember that decision-making requires us to invest cognitive resources, so the more our guiding principles direct our decisions, the less we need to tap our decision-making energies. Furthermore, when our guiding principles support what really matters then doing the right thing becomes almost automatic.

> *"When our guiding principles support what really matters then doing the right thing becomes almost automatic."*

You already do this. If you're a non-smoker who values good health and fitness then the decision whether to light up a cigarette each hour doesn't vex you. If you're happily married to a wonderful person who completes you then I'm willing to bet you're not now weighing the pros and cons of running off to Vegas with a stranger. Speaking for myself, I can't remember the last time I robbed a bank. This isn't because each morning I wake up and think to myself, "Is this the day I hold up Wells Fargo?" It's because at some point I established a guiding principle that took that option off the table. In other words, by making one value-based decision I established a default setting on thousands of little decisions for the rest of my life.

Businesses practice this as well, some more deliberately than others. In their book, *Buck Up, Suck Up...and Come Back When You Foul Up: 12 Winning Secrets from the War Room*, James Carville and Paul Begal share Herb Kelleher's (Southwest's longest-serving CEO) description of the airlines guiding principle:

> *"I can teach you the secret to running this airline in 30 seconds. This is it: We are THE low-fare airline. Once you understand that fact, you can make any decision about this company's future as well as I can."*[1]

With a little thought experiment we can see for ourselves how this might work. Take for example Ben & Jerry's. Some of their guiding principles include:

▶ Fairtrade, helping small farmers in developing countries compete and thrive in the global economy.

▶ Working toward world peace and ending the wasteful spending on more and more weapons systems.

▶ Ending social injustice and reducing the gap between the rich and the poor.

▶ Putting a stop to the use of recombinant bovine growth hormone (rBGH) and genetically-modified foods (GMO).[2]

Now, imagine we're on the board of Ben & Jerry's, and in the lobby are two men, each with a business proposition. In walks the first person. Sharp dressed, clean shaven, he says he has a compelling business opportunity for us to consider. He points out that our ice cream is very expensive and so sales are lower than they could be otherwise. What's more, we use very expensive ingredients so our profit margins are thin. All this means we don't make as much money as we could and so are limited in our ability to make the world a better place. So here's his proposal: he tells us he can supply us with milk and eggs at pennies on the dollar. He can do this because state-owned dairy farms in North Korea using rBGH and GMO farming practices are eager to find buyers for their goods. By sourcing from North Korea we can lower the cost of our ice cream. This would increase sales. What's more, lower cost ingredients would also see our profit margin shoot up. It's a no-brainer!

So what do we say? Well, if we use the company's guiding principles as a map then there's no discussion to be had. Fairtrade? World peace? Social injustice? GMO? The proposal is a non-starter. We politely show the man the door and wait for the second proposal.

In walks the second man. The dude looks like he walked here via the Appalachian Trail. He apologizes for taking our time and promises to keep his presentation short. He represents a small commune deep in the Vermont countryside that's hard at work establishing an organic dairy. The commune is located on a newly-completed superfund site, one that had recently been returned to its pristine condition after years of military use. They're new and struggling, so they can't offer us very competitive prices. In fact, it might be a little on the high side, even by our standards. In part this is because the commune wants to provide healthcare and other social benefits for all of its employees and their families.

How do you think the board of Ben & Jerry's would respond? We can't say for sure, but my guess is they'd say, "Tell us more." You see where I'm going. Of course we don't sit on the board of Ben & Jerry's, but using their guiding principles as a map, we can be pretty darn sure how they would decide in these two instances. No investment of cognitive resources necessary.

Discover Your Guiding Principles

The good news is when it comes to defining our guiding principles, it's not exactly like we're starting from scratch. Our upbringing, life experiences, the culture in which we were raised, our religious background, education, economic conditions, accomplishments—all these things greatly inform our perspectives on life. What's left for us to do is to take the time to discover what these values are and see if they really are ours.

For example, years ago my father was helping me finish my basement. (Well, when I say helping me, I mean to say I was helping him. What? Okay. When I say I was helping him, I mean to say I was getting in the way. But I digress.) Now when it comes to construction, my father is no slouch, but as is the case when remodeling a home or adding on a room, things would invariably go wrong. Yet whenever they did, he would simply say, "There's always a solution." The meaning was clear: There's a problem? No big whoop. There's always a solution, so no need to get all wrapped around the axel. Because of this guiding principle my father rarely if ever lost his cool. (Sure, he'd drop the tools, walk away for a few minutes, and have a glass of wine, but hey, that's just wise allocation of his cognitive resources.) This sentiment, *there's always a solution*, stuck with me over the years and has guided the way I approach my own work in just about every aspect.

How Many Values Should You Have?

It may be tempting to set some arbitrary number so we can feel like we've hit the mark and can move forward, but the number isn't nearly as important as the relevance and honesty of the values:

▶ **Relevance:** As we mentioned earlier, our upbringing, culture, religious background, education, and economic conditions already give us a ready-made set of values, but the vast majority are not immediately relevant to our desire to perform with intent. For example, if you're from the United States, odds are you like about three feet of personal space when speaking with others. You value your personal space, but is that relevant to what you're trying to accomplish? Not really. Not unless you're trying to decide what career path to follow and you come from a long line of massage therapists. We should list those values that will guide us toward the sort of life we want to lead.

▶ **Honesty:** This may sound easier than it really is. Discovering our values requires us to be honest with who we are and what drives our behaviors and passions. This can be problematic if our personal values run counter to those around us. Consider the Amish tradition of *Rumspringa* in which, upon turning 16, Amish youths go off to experience the world of the "English." During this time the kids run wild (some wilder than others) then decide whether the life of the Amish is for them.[3] During this time the pressure felt to return to the community is probably tremendous. Some may have no real interest in living the Amish lifestyle but nevertheless feel a strong need to return for the community, family, tradition, etc. Many may wish they felt the way their families did—tell themselves that surely, in time, they'd come to love the austere life as much as the others—but deep down inside know it's not for them. In these cases, personal honesty has to trump community, family, or personal pressures.

Your Moral and Ethical Autopilot

There will be no shortage of situations in which the proverbial angel and devil will take up residence on our shoulders and try to persuade us toward one direction or another. Times like these will not only vex us but will cost us cognitive resources. Having strong, value-based guiding principles that support our sense of meaning and purpose will serve as kind of a moral and ethical autopilot. They'll guide our behavior without missing a beat, taking us down that path that most enhances our life's purpose.

Values Evolve

It's inevitable that our values will evolve and shift over time. A quote often attributed to Winston Churchill (probably erroneously so—Churchill was conservative from day-one) goes as follows: "If you're not a liberal when you're 25, you have no heart. If you're not a conservative by the time you're 35, you have no brain." Despite the questionable origin of the phrase, the message is provocative. Values, principles, and ideals that guide our thoughts and behaviors evolve over time. Speaking for myself, I would be somewhat skeptical of someone who, at the age of 50, holds to the same values as he or she had at 15. Life is a wonderful journey of growth and learning. Evolution is not only inevitable but desirable. Ossified values are not a virtue; they show a lack of openness to learning and growth.

In Summary

1. **Values guide your behavior:** Your values act as guiding principles in your life, rationalizing the rightness and wrongness of what you encounter and the decisions you make.

2. **You are already following guiding principles:** Your upbringing, the culture in which you were raised, your religious background, education, economic conditions, accomplishments—all these things have already greatly informed your perspective on life.

3. **Guiding principles reduce the need to invest cognitive resources:** Guiding principles can replace the need for earnest deliberation and decision-making in many of life's more vexing moments.

4. **Relevance and honesty are key:** The number of values is not nearly as important as their relevance and honesty.

5. **Values evolve:** As life's journey educates your understanding of yourself and those around you, your guiding principles and values will evolve.

Your Turn

Guiding principles constitute the foundation of the ADEPT Model, so it's important to take the time to really understand what principles drive your actions and decisions. So what are your guiding principles? Pull out your notebook and let's see if we can't get at the core of what makes you tick:

▶ What are the behaviors you admire most, that you aspire to embody?

_____

_____

_____

_____

_____

_____

_____

_____

▶ What are the behaviors you admire least, that you frown upon and eschew?

_____

_____

_____

_____

_____

_____

_____

► How do you want to be thought of, remembered, and talked about?

_____

_____

_____

_____

_____

_____

_____

_____

► If you could give a loved one life advice before this person were to leave for a long journey, what would you say? Think of Polonius as he spoke with his son Laertes in Shakespeare's *Hamlet*. "My blessing with thee! And these few precepts in thy memory." He then went on to say such things as, "Give thy thoughts no tongue," "Neither a borrower nor a lender be," and "This above all: to thine ownself be true." What would your words of wisdom be, and how do they reflect your values?

_____

_____

_____

_____

_____

_____

_____

_____

We're going to refer back to these principles frequently, so set yourself up for success and jot down your thoughts.

2. Passion

One day an organizational director brought her senior staff together for a three-day conference. To help kick things off she asked the dozen or so attendees this question: if you didn't have to earn a living, what would you do with your time? A simple icebreaker question, but the answers were illuminating. Many said they would work for a charitable cause or dedicate their time to some philanthropic effort. One said she wanted to write a book about what it was like to be adopted and meeting her birthmother. Another wanted to write a self-help book for parents struggling to raise a handicapped child. The responses all varied, but after a while a theme began to emerge: people wanted to spend their time doing something they felt had meaning and could make a difference.

It may be interesting to note that no one said they would be a senior-level manager in a global high-tech corporation—exactly what they all were.

Like all of us, these staff members wanted to feel a sense of purpose in what they did. They needed to feel like what they did mattered—and consequently that they mattered. Even though these folks were at the height of their careers and were all well compensated, this didn't make up for the lack of purpose many of them seemed to feel.

All of us have things that get us out of bed in the morning and give us the courage and determination to take on another day. The question is, do we have a good understanding of what these things are and how to prioritize them when our finite resources become scarce? Everyone in this story had a good understanding what gave them purpose and meaning, but like the rest of us, they had to balance their passions, obligations, and commitments.

Tapping Your Intrinsic Motivation

Do you have a hobby, or maybe something you enjoy doing simply for the sheer enjoyment of it? Reading a good book? Art? Sports? Maybe you enjoy painting, creating stained glass, or working on cars. It could be you're one of the millions of golfers, runners, or cyclists who can hardly wait to get out the door and play. Now tell me, how much are you paid to read books, cycle 50 miles, or hit a round of golf? If you're like most of us, you're not. In fact, chances are *you pay others* for the privilege of participating in these activities—sometimes a lot! And that's just the financial investment. Many spend a great deal of time and energy on such interests.

This sort of passionate dedication to an activity is fed by *intrinsic motivation*. When we say we're motivated or rewarded intrinsically we're saying we do it for "the love of the game," because it's who we are, how we express ourselves, and how we discover who we are in this crazy thing called life. *Extrinsic motivation*, by contrast, comes not from within us but from sources outside. Extrinsic rewards include money, benefits, awards, or the threat of losing these things. We've all heard the saying, "You couldn't pay me to do that." Well extrinsic motivation says, "Gee, are you sure?" We all need money to survive so we give of ourselves, our time, energy, and talents to earn our way through life. But often this means doing things for which we have little intrinsic interest. We do it for the paycheck, and that's it. Think of it this way:

Extrinsic motivation says, "I'll do it if you pay me."

Intrinsic motivation says, "I'll pay you if you let me do it."

Discovering our passion means discovering what energizes us intrinsically. But what are the ingredients to this magical state; one in which we'd be willing to pay others for the privileged of doing something? Our sense of intrinsic motivation increases when we feel a sense of autonomy, competence, relatedness, and achievement in what we do.[1, 2, 3, 4]

So what does this mean? Well, we feel a sense of autonomy when we believe that what we're doing is rooted in our own values, goals, needs, and interests (as opposed to those of some unnamable external source).[5] For instance, as a college professor I have the autonomy to teach my classes the way I feel best fits my style, approach, values, interests, and the needs of my students. I'm given the leeway to make the class my own.

Competence is brought about by a feeling of efficacy in the environment as we exercise our craft.[6] In other words, competency tells us we rock, that we crush it! It drives us to seek after new challenges that use and enhance the skills and abilities that define our sense of competence.[7] Once again using my role as professor as an example, I'm pretty good at what I do. After 30 years in corporate America, an MBA, a Ph.D., access to some of the best minds in business, and strong teaching skills, I feel I have the competence to bring true value to the classroom.

Relatedness is the need to establish close personal bonds and relationships with others, allowing us to find emotional and caring support and security.[8] As a professor I get to work with some of the best minds out there—learned accomplished faculty and eager students who remind me that life is pretty darn exciting and worth exploring each and every day.

Finally, we gain a great deal of intrinsic satisfaction when we achieve something that has purpose and meaning to us.[9] In my case, teaching a class and seeing a student embrace what I have to offer is an achievement that can feed me for some time.

If we have the chance to act in accordance with our values, have the skills to be effective, have the chance to develop deep and nurturing relationships with others, and have the opportunity apply all this to accomplishing something meaningful, we're going to be highly intrinsically motivated (and probably uber-successful to boot!).

Size Doesn't Matter

On December 10, 1997, Julia "Butterfly" Hill climbed a 180-foot, 1500-year-old California Redwood to protect it from loggers. What she thought would be a two or three week peaceful protest turned into a 738-day odyssey, one which included harassment from helicopters, a ten-day siege by company security guards, and protests from angry loggers. All this while being pummeled by freezing rains and 40 mph winds. Still, she held fast (literally and figuratively) and in the end was able to save the tree and many more in the region.[10]

Now to you or me the idea of spending two years in a tree may seem a tad excessive. I mean, there are something in the neighborhood of three trillions trees on Earth.[11] Does investing so much of oneself in a single tree really make sense? Well that's my point. Things that give us meaning and purpose don't need to make sense. Traveling all over the country to show off one's prize Pomeranian in hopes of winning a blue ribbon? Not me. Searching back 27 generations to do family genealogy? No thanks. But that's okay. Not everything has to be meaningful to everyone.

> "Something doesn't have to have meaning and purpose to give us meaning and purpose."

The thing that's so great about society is we all benefit from the passions of others. We enjoy amazing art and music, incredible technology, great books beyond number, national parks and open space, thriving economies and civil government, all thanks to the passions of others. So don't worry if what gives you meaning may seem small or mundane in the vast scheme of things. Something doesn't have to *have* meaning and purpose to *give* us meaning and purpose.

But a word of caution: the reverse holds true as well. Just because something *gives* us meaning doesn't mean it *has* meaning. We need to be careful that we don't become that person who believes that what gives us meaning trumps all other causes. These people don't get invited to many parties. Purpose and meaning are not properties intrinsically held by objects or activities. Rather, we imbue activities with the importance we see in them. What to you or me may seem relatively trivial, to others may be what gets them up in the morning. (More about this later.)

In Summary

1. **Your passion is what gets you up in the morning:** Your sense of intrinsic motivation increases when you feel a sense of autonomy, competence, relatedness, and achievement in what you do.

2. **Passion is the measure; not size or impact:** The strength of your passion isn't in its size or its potential to have significant impact in the world. It lies in its ability to fire you up and inspire you to act.

3. **Just because something *gives* you meaning and purpose doesn't mean it *has* meaning and purpose:** What's important to you may not be important to someone else, and that's okay.

Your Turn

Now that you have an idea of what contributes to someone's passion, let's see if we can home in on what turns your crank. Ask yourself the following questions and see what sort of patterns emerge:

▶ As a child, what did you want to be when you grew up? Why was that exciting to you?

_____

_____

_____

_____

_____

_____

_____

▶ What would you do if you knew there was no way you could fail?

_____

_____

_____

_____

_____

_____

_____

▶ What would you do with your time if there was no need to earn a living?

_____

_____

_____

_____

_____

_____

_____

_____

▶ What would you do if you knew you only had five years to live?

_____

_____

_____

_____

_____

_____

_____

_____

▶ What are you good at, not necessarily because you're well-trained, but because you just plain love doing it?

_____

_____

_____

_____

_____

_____

_____

_____

▶ What sort of people do you enjoy hanging out with? Craftsmen? Business professionals? Academics? Children? Parents? Athletes? Entrepreneurs? Social workers? What does this say about you?

_____

_____

_____

_____

_____

_____

_____

► What achievements are you most proud of, and why?

_____

_____

_____

_____

_____

_____

_____

_____

Passion is what gets you up in the morning with a spring in your step, makes you look forward to the day ahead, gets you excited for what may come next, and gives you the courage to tackle new and exciting challenges. Clearly, understanding your passions is paramount!

3. Strengths and Weaknesses

I hesitate to bring up strengths and weaknesses. Research has shown we are happiest when we feel like we know what we're doing. In other words, if we're good at something then we'll like doing it, and in turn increase our odds of success. Based on this it makes good sense to explore our strengths (and since we're in this very section right now, you already know we're going to). The problem is this: what happens when our passions—those things that give us purpose and meaning—require skills that we have no hope of ever developing? Does that mean we'll never feel fulfilled? Not necessarily.

In his book, *StrenthsFinder 2.0*, author Tom Rath takes a new twist on the story of Rudy Ruettiger, the inspiration for the 1993 movie *Rudy*. Ever since he was young all Rudy could think about was playing football for Notre Dame. Problem is, at five-foot-six and 165 pounds, Rudy didn't strike a typical footballer's pose. Academically he wasn't much better. Notre Dame rejected him three times before finally admitting him to the university. Eventually he earned a spot on the football team's practice squad. In essence his job was to take beatings. This went on for two years. During that time he never once suited up to join the team on the sidelines, let alone on the field. Until, that is, for the last game of his senior year. In the final few minutes of a game that had been pretty much sewn up by the regular team, Rudy was

> *"What makes someone successful goes beyond a simple return-on-investment quotient."*

allowed to take the field. After years or taking beatings on the practice squad, Rudy rose to the challenge and sacked the opposing team's quarterback. The crowd went wild, tears were shed, and a legend was born.

Stories don't come much more inspirational than that, but then Rath points something out. "While Rudy's perseverance is admirable, in the end, he played a few seconds of college football and made a single tackle…after thousands of hours of practicing." Rath goes on to suggest that had Rudy dedicated that same level of passion and hard work to something he was actually *good* at, imagine how successful he might have been.[1]

Now I've never met Rudy Ruettiger, but my guess is the man never once thought how successful he *might* have been. He achieved his dream. How much more successful can one be? I appreciate where Rath is coming from, and from a strengths and weaknesses perspective alone, he's absolutely right. Rudy was predestined to fail as a football player. However, what makes someone successful goes beyond a simple return-on-investment quotient. True, considering the amount of time, effort, and passion Rudy put into his venture, a successful play or two is a pretty poor return on his investment. But as you and I already know, those things that give us meaning and purpose don't give a rat's patootie about return on investment. So what if Rudy was only successful for a few seconds? For those few moments he was a god. When was the last time you were a god?

Rudy's lesson is an important one: we don't have to be the best in the world at something to find purpose and meaning in the activity. In fact, we don't even have to be any good at it.

> *"We don't have to be the best in the world at something to find purpose and meaning in the activity. In fact, we don't even have to be any good at it."*

Despite my reservations with Rath's analogy, his focus on strengths is not without merit and should play an important role in discovering our own purpose. Understanding our strengths and weaknesses helps us prioritize our lives and opens up the best chances for success in the scope of our passions.

"Think how successful you might have been had you done something you're good at!"

Strengths Make Opportunities Possible / Weaknesses Expose You to Threats

As we noted earlier, we're only as free as our resources allow. Just because a jet aircraft is for sale doesn't mean I have the opportunity to buy and fly it. Only those with the resources can truly say they have the opportunity. Our strengths follow the same rule. There may be an opening on the Olympic track and field team, but that doesn't mean I have the opportunity to compete. I don't have the speed, the access to coaches, the connections to get my name on the list, the ability to recover from the arduous workouts—you name it; I don't have it. Now yes, if this is all I ever wanted in my life then I could maybe pull some sort of Rudy move and be involved at some level, but then I'd be drawing on different strengths: grit, determination, passion, heart, willingness to realign my definition of success to meet what was really possible, and so forth.

All this brings me to my point: our strengths make opportunities possible. If you're a gifted public speaker and a speaking opportunity comes up, then you're set. But now let's extend that. What if someone invites you to participate in open mic night at a comedy club? You're good at public speaking, so yeah, maybe this is something to explore. You see? Your strength as a speaker makes an opportunity a genuine possibility.

What about on the weakness side of the equation? Well, just as our strengths make opportunities possible, our weaknesses expose us to threats. Think of it this way: someone with a weakened immune system is more susceptible to the threat of infection than someone with a fully-functioning immune system. This means the person with the deficient system needs to take measures to mitigate the threat of contracting an illness.

Beware of Your Blind Spot

Taking a microscope to our weaknesses can hardly be considered a barrel of monkeys. All things being equal, we'd just assume not give our weaknesses a whole lot of thought. Furthermore, odds are we're not fully aware of many of our vulnerabilities. They exist in our blind spot—that place where we can't see clearly and tend not to check. Honest self-examination is the key. But also, remember this: the reason we identify our weaknesses is not to show us how sure we are to fail but to put systems and processes in place to mitigate them. We identify our weaknesses so we can eliminate them or reduce their effect. You can't defuse a bomb if you don't look for it or ignore it.

Context Decides Strengths and Weaknesses

Simply being good or poor at something doesn't make it a strength or a weakness. It all depends on what you hope to accomplish—your 'X.' For example, Michael Jordan's height worked in his favor as he developed into one of the greatest basketball players in history. However, that same height would have been a liability had he wanted to become a horse jockey in the Kentucky Derby. The trait alone—in this case height—has no intrinsic value. It's not until we look at the context that we can decide whether something is a strength or a weakness.

In Summary

1. **Strengths make opportunities possible:** It's only an opportunity if you have the skills, resources, and passion to exploit the opportunity.

2. **Weaknesses expose you to threats:** When you lack the skills, resources, and passions to accomplish something, you set yourself up for failure.

3. **Beware of your blind spot:** Be willing to look in the uncomfortable places to identify weaknesses. Only then can you defuse their potential to do you harm and mitigate their effect.

4. **Context decides strengths and weaknesses:** Your 'X' decides whether a skill or attribute is a strength or a weakness.

Your Turn

Think about the passions you identified in the previous section. With these in mind, ask yourself what skills or abilities you bring to the party, or perhaps lack. This will point you in the direction of your strengths and weaknesses. Remember, you're only interested in understanding those strengths and weaknesses that are germane to your purpose. Me, I can't play a musical instrument to save my life, but since this has absolutely nothing to do with my passion it's not a weakness I need to worry myself over. On the other hand, I'm pretty good at explaining complex things in a way that most people can easily understand. As a teacher, this is definitely a strength I can mark up in the plus column. So now you try:

Strengths

▶   What can you do, maybe better than most?

_____

_____

_____

_____

_____

_____

_____

_____

▶ What are you known for among your friends, family, and co-workers?

_____

_____

_____

_____

_____

_____

_____

_____

▶ What accomplishments are you particularly proud of? What skills or
   abilities did you bring to the table that made these successes possible?

_____

_____

_____

_____

_____

_____

_____

_____

Weaknesses

▶ What skills do you feel like you lack; abilities you feel are important to pursing your passion?

_____

_____

_____

_____

_____

_____

_____

_____

▶ What sort of constructive feedback, coaching, or criticism have you received from your friends, family, and co-workers?

_____

_____

_____

_____

_____

_____

_____

▶ What skills do you lack that have prevented you from succeeding at some
point in the past?

_____

_____

_____

_____

_____

_____

_____

_____

Be careful you don't sell yourself short; you have many impressive strengths.
Likewise, be careful you don't gloss over your weaknesses. Nothing can
sabotage performance like an overlooked weakness. Underestimate them at
your own peril!

4. Support from Others

Many years ago I worked as an operations manager for an internal HR communications organization. One day my director asked me to develop a way for us to track and measure what we did with data so we could better tell our story to the leadership team. I wasn't exactly a metrics expert, but I knew communications and had an appreciation for data and operational excellence. I also agreed we needed to find a way to better demonstrate our value, so I accepted the challenge and set to work. I did my homework, found the best practices the industry had to offer, engaged with key team members and influencers, won the support of the organizational leader, and designed something I thought would meet our needs nicely. Everything was ready to go, so then it was time to roll out the final product and supporting processes to the entire team.

I began to explain what everyone would have to do and how the data would be gathered and reported. However, as I spoke it became clear the team wasn't having any of it. They vociferously challenged the value of the data and the processes required to collect it. As they continued to debate the merits of my proposal I realized there wasn't even agreement on what sort of data the team should track or why. They began to argue over roles, who would be responsible for gathering what sort of data, and what we should be done with the information.

In the end my metrics package failed to catch on, and I had only myself to blame. I hadn't gained sufficient stakeholder support, and without support the plan was dead on arrival. It was a difficult lesson for me to learn, but one which I think back on regularly. Ever since then, when people talk about the importance of support from others, I give them an emphatic "Amen!"

Many people (including myself at the time) mistakenly view winning support from others as an objective—something we work on doing as part of our journey to success. But it makes more sense to view support from others as a constraint—something that will torpedo our goals if we fail to take it into account. People who don't win support from others fail, pure and simple. Just in that not everything in the world is important and worthy of our finite resources, there's no guarantee that what's important to us will have the same level of importance—

"People that don't win support from others fail, pure and simple."

indeed, any importance at all—to our stakeholders. Like us, they have to constantly weigh where they're going to lend their support and where they're going to cut lose. This means we need to deliver something of value in return for their support. If a stakeholder doesn't perceive value in what we're doing they won't lend their support, and without their support, we're dead in the water.[1]

Who Are Your Supporters?

A supporter is anyone with a vested interest in our success. To put it another way, supporters are people and organizations who invest their own resources in us so we might be successful, presumably so they can then benefit from that success. For example:

▶ Creditors lend us money (their resources) in the hopes our success will pay them a return on their investment (the benefit).

▶ Families give up time to be with us (their resources) in the hopes our success will result in financial opportunity for the family (the benefit).

▶ A community represented by a city government gives us a building permit to remodel our home (its resources) in the hopes our success will raise property values in the area (the benefit).

▶ An employer gives us a compensation package (its resources) in the hopes our success will generate additional profits for the company (the benefit).

▶ An employee give us her commitment and very best effort (her resources) in the hopes our success will open up career opportunities for her in the future (the benefit).

When we think about it, we need the support of dozens if not hundreds of stakeholders to be successful.

Supporters Help to Fill Your Resources Gaps

For every person's victory there's an army of supporters who helped make it happen. It doesn't matter how much passion, genius, or work ethic Neil Armstrong might have had. Without hundreds of engineers and a country of citizens supporting his efforts, Armstrong never would have set foot on the moon. One of the reasons Julia "Butterfly" Hill was able to last so long atop her 1500-year-old redwood was because she had tremendous support from those who believed in her cause. There's no way she could have survived in the branches of that tree for 738 days without constant fanatical support from an eight-member support crew.[2] Food, supplies, oversight—without these supporters Julia wouldn't have lasted a week.

Supporters provide us with innumerable types of nourishment. From tangible resources and skills to emotional support and encouragement, supporters are the lifeblood of any successful venture. They can also help us overcome some of the weaknesses we identified earlier. For example, every now and again my wife needs to pull together a PowerPoint presentation, trifold brochure, or some other collateral material for her employer. She's a tremendously talented artist, but computer graphics aren't her thing. Me, I have the creativity of a small stone, but I know graphic design. I can channel a past life as a layout artist and whip out a brochure in minutes. With me as a supporter of her professional career, all she needs to do it bat her eyes, tell me how smart and talented I am, and BAM! She's got her brochure. Skills gap filled.

Support Should Never Be Assumed

Stakeholders are comprised of different people, groups, and organizations, each with their criteria for evaluating how well we're meeting their expectations. After all, everyone has a different interest in the outcome. Faced with conflicting demands, we have to decide which relationships need nurturing.[3] This means that we need to assess and prioritize how we address the needs of our supporters.

That said, support from others is by no means a given. Everyone around us is busy allocating their own limited resources to their own passions and priorities. We should be grateful when our goals align with theirs and they choose to support us. It should never be something we take for granted.

But what about family or employees, you might ask? Our families pretty much have to support us, right? Filial piety, Confucius might call it. As far as employees are concerned, they know it's either support the goal or find another job. So can't it be said that some support is sort of built-in?

Yeah, sure. Let me know how that works out for you.

Just as we bring more energy and passion to that which we believe in intrinsically, so do our supporters. The more someone feels like an indentured servant to what seems like a pointless or arbitrary cause, the less support we'll receive. So trust me when I say no one's support should ever be assumed or taken for granted.

Supporters Need to Be Fed

After we successfully win over our supporters we need to give them regular care and feeding. The last thing we want them to feel is that we're taking them for granted or wasting their resources. Later we'll talk about what we can do to keep our supporters engaged and cheering for our success, but for now, know there's a world of difference between *winning* support and *maintaining* support. We'll discuss both at length.

In Summary

1. **Without support from others you will fail:** You can't succeed without the help, support, and encouragement of others.

2. **Stakeholders fill skills and resource gaps:** No one person possesses every skill and resource needed accomplish great things, but that's okay. Those who believe in what you're doing can help fill the gaps.

3. **Support from others should never be assumed:** The moment you take the contributions and support from others for granted marks the beginning of your monumental fail.

Your Turn

Supporters are often the unsung heroes of many great accomplishments. That being the case, it's a good idea to understand who they are, what moves them, and how they would like us to sing their praises. Take a few minutes and jot down the following:

▶ Who have been your supporters in the past?

_____

_____

_____

_____

_____

_____

_____

_____

▶ How has their support meant the difference between success and failure for you in the past?

_____

_____

_____

_____

_____

_____

_____

_____

▶ What do these people hope to receive in return for their support?

_____

_____

_____

_____

_____

_____

_____

_____

▶ On the other side of the equation, who are your naysayers—those who have sought to discourage you?

_____

_____

_____

_____

_____

_____

_____

_____

► Why do you think these folks have been hesitant to lend you their support?

_____

_____

_____

_____

_____

_____

_____

_____

► What can you do to win them over?

_____

_____

_____

_____

_____

_____

_____

_____

Trust me, your supporters are going to be integral to any goal you set for yourself. Taking the time now to understand what makes them tick will pay dividends in the future.

5. Supporting Infrastructure

Many civil servants like to focus on providing things like roads, bridges, water, electricity, and public transit systems. Why? Because these people understand that a sound and robust infrastructure is critical to building and sustaining economic growth. They help attract talent, create business investment, and allow for the transport of goods, both locally and globally.[1] If you're pro-economic development then there's a better than even chance you're pro-infrastructure as well. It's pretty intuitive when you think about it. Not many people would be interested in building a home where there's no water, sewage, electricity, gas, roads, schools, hospitals, and so on. A supporting infrastructure makes it easier to do those things that are necessary for success.

Just as a country, state, or city needs a strong infrastructure to facilitate growth and prosperity, so also do we need structures that enable us to perform with intent. Let me show you what I mean.

For close to a decade now I've had a 1965 MG Midget in my garage up on blocks and in complete disarray. (My wife calls it my *garage decoration*.) Over the years I've put maybe 100 hours into it. In that same time I earned a Ph.D., completed my fourth Ironman, started a consulting business, published two books, and started teaching at a local college. So what's the deal? Why haven't I made any progress on this ridiculous thing taking up space in my garage? It would be tempting to say it must not be that important to me, but I don't think that's entirely true. This car represents an important part of me, something I want to develop and nurture. So what is it then? It's the lack of an infrastructure and the amount of concerted effort necessary to be successful. For example, let's compare my eight-to-five job with my MG Midget project:

Schedule

▶ **My Job:** It's from eight to five, Monday through Friday. Boom. Scheduling done. Zero thought required.

▶ **My MG:** Scheduling time to hunker down and work on the blasted thing takes concerted planning and effort.

Support from Others

▶ **My Job:** Everyone knows the job is from eight to five, Monday through Friday. My family won't look at me as I prepare to head into the office and say, "Do you have to do this now?" Heading off to work in the morning and coming home in the evening is a built-in cultural norm.

▶ **My MG:** Taking time to work on the MG means taking time away from others—folks who have already given up a lot of my time as I work to earn a living. They can see their way to allowing me a little time now and again, but it's hard to sustain.

Access to Tools and Resources

▶ **My Job:** When I get to work I have access to the tools and resources I need to be successful. Computers, systems, material, connectivity—you name it; I've got it.

▶ **My MG:** I have a few wrenches (spanners I suppose, since it's a British car) and a hammer somewhere. Oh, and some screwdrivers, but that's about the extent of it. A far cry from all the specialized tools needed to work on a classic British sports car.

Competence and Expertise

▶ **My Job:** I know how to do my job and how to do it well. I have close to 30 years' experience. I've gone to university and collected an assortment of hoity-toity letters after my name. If I need additional training I know where to get it.

▶ **My MG:** I don't know the first thing about how to approach this heap of parts. Wires, gears, motors, bodywork—and what's this thingamajig?! It's completely hopeless.

Facilities

▶ **My Job:** The office environment itself is conducive to doing the task at hand. I have an ergonomically-correct workspace designed to promote maximum productivity.

▶ **My MG:** I have a cramped garage that I share with my family. Littered all about are bicycles, gardening tools, cans of paint, bits of wood here and there, some drywall we can't bring ourselves to toss out, bundles of wire, camping gear, and anything else you can imagine.

Accountability

▶ **My Job:** At work I have leaders and customers to whom I'm accountable. If I don't deliver then there are consequences. It's my derrière on the line.

▶ **My MG:** There's no one looking at my schedule, wondering when the heck I'm going to get this car running. Sure, my wife occasionally makes the stray comment, but she's exceedingly patient with me. At the end of the day I'm accountable to no one. This may seem like a good thing, but few things are more effective than deadlines and accountability when it comes to getting things done.

Experts and Mentors

▶ **My Job:** Over the years I've had the good fortune to meet many experts in my field who can help me think through and solve business problems. No matter the challenge, odds are I know someone who's had to tackle the same issue. A phone call and maybe a lunch later and I have the beginnings of a solution.

▶ **My MG:** There simply aren't that many people who have the masochistic tendency necessary to take on such a project. British sports cars are notoriously difficult to get up and running. Most folks I know prefer to stick with American muscle, and for good reason. Sure, I have the Internet, but that's no substitution for someone standing next to me, showing me how to approach a problem.

As you can see, my day job has all the ingredients I need to be successful. The '65 MG Midget, on the other hand, is all but doomed to fail. (Why then am I still hanging on to thing? Hey, I never said I had the ADEPT Model 100% dialed in myself.) The higher the level of concerted effort required, the more it'll tax our ability to see it through.

Structure Is Your Friend—and Your Enemy

As the example above illustrates, a supporting structure can mean the difference between tremendous success and dismal failure. However, this presumes our structures point us in the right direction. This may not necessarily be the case. Some structures may actually inhibit us from performing with intent. For example, those suffering from an addiction may find their structures enable their self-destructive behavior. Friends, family, an environment that encourages drug use—all these structural factors can

> *"A supporting structure can mean the difference between tremendous success and dismal failure."*

hinder their ability to overcome the addiction.[2] In the same way, many of our structures may be preventing us from reaching our full potential. A good friend of mine had a TV and video game console in his office. I mentioned this to my wife and she came back with an immediate, "Well you're not getting one!" My friend saw the gaming system as a way to now and again take a quick break and decompress. My wife, on the other hand, knew better. She understood that having a gaming system in the office would pull me away from the task at hand.

In Summary

1. **The lack of structures makes it hard to do anything:** It's hard to bring yourself to do anything when it's not scheduled, supported, or resourced.

2. **The right structures make it easy to do the right things:** It's easy to do something when it's scheduled, supported, and resourced—and that's good when it means performing with intent.

3. **The wrong structures make it easy to do the wrong things:** It's easy to do something when it's scheduled, supported, and resourced—and that's bad when it prevents us from performing with intent.

Your Turn

Later we'll talk about how to develop structures that can help you achieve what matters. Right now though let's consider what structures you currently have in place, which one's may be missing, and what they enable or prevent you from doing. To that end, consider the following questions:

▶ How does your current schedule help or hinder you?

_____

_____

_____

_____

_____

_____

_____

_____

▶ What tools and resources do you need to be successful? Do you have everything you need, or are some things missing?

_____

_____

_____

_____

_____

_____

_____

_____

▶ Do you have access to the expertise necessary to succeed? What about experts and mentors?

_____

_____

_____

_____

_____

_____

_____

▶ Do you have access to the facilities necessary to succeed?

_____

_____

_____

_____

_____

_____

_____

▶ What accountability structures do you have in place? Do you have deadlines? To whom are you accountable? What are the consequences if you miss a deadline?

The presence of supporting structures can almost make success something of a foregone conclusion. On the other hand, the absence of such structures will make anything you try infinitely more difficult. Now's a good time to think about what you have in place and what you may be missing.

So Here's a Thought...

You walk into a room. Inside are all the tools, equipment, facilities, and supplies you need to be successful. We're talking top of the line; the best money can buy. What's in that room? Now, imagine that someone comes in and one by one points to each item and says you can't have this, but then asks is there something you have that will allow you to get by. After you're all done, do you have enough of what you need to at least get started? What might still be missing? Is it the lack of resources that's holding you back or the lack of courage to get started?

CHAPTER 5: ELIMINATE
(what doesn't matter)

You gotta to put down the ducky if you want to play the saxophone.

– Hoots the Owl, Sesame Street

Muppet

French aviator and author of *Le Petit Prince*, Antoine de Saint-Exupéry, said in his book, *Airman's Odyssey*, "Perfection is achieved, not when there is nothing more to add, but when there is nothing left to take away." Later I'm going to go on a little tirade when it comes to the word *perfection*, but for now let's just step back and appreciate the minimalist simplicity of this quote. All too often it seems like we're trying to add more and more to our lives, thinking this will make them easier, when in fact it's just the opposite.

Writers understand this principle. In writing circles there's a phrase that invariably comes up at some point during the editing process:

"Kill your darlings."

Arthur Quiller-Couch, one of the preeminent early twentieth-century literary experts, railed against what he called "extraneous ornament." He said, "Whenever you feel an impulse to perpetrate a piece of exceptionally fine writing, obey it—whole-heartedly—and delete it before sending your manuscript to press. Murder your darlings."[1] In his book, *On Writing*, Stephen King wrote, "Kill your darlings, kill your darlings, even when it breaks your egocentric little scribbler's heart, kill your darlings."[2] The "darlings" to which these authors are referring are their words—the stock and trade of the craft. Writers have a particular relationship with words, one that inspires perhaps undue levels of reverence and pride of authorship. "Killing your darlings" means cut, cut, and then, when you think you can't cut anymore, cut again. It hurts because we writers enjoy the delusion that what we write has value, but as the adage goes, less is more, so we eliminate the fat to get to the core of our narratives.

And so now it's our turn to kill our darlings.

We've come to a greater understanding of our guiding principles. We've identified those things that feed our passions. With this as a context we've taken the time to consider our strengths and weaknesses. We've given thought to who might help support us in our endeavors, and what we need to do to win and keep their support. Finally, we've assessed the structures we have in place, the structures that may be missing, and how these structures are directing or misdirecting our efforts. With all this sorted it's time to separate the wheat from the chaff. This means *Eliminating* those things in our lives that are not driving us in the right direction.

It goes without saying that this is easier said than done. Some of these things are our darlings. But make no mistake, *Eliminating* the things standing in our way is one of the most important steps in the ADEPT Model. The three economic laws of performing with intent have already taught us that we can't do everything, so it's time to decide what gets done and what gets dumped. Think of it as a self-imposed hoarding intervention. Over the years we've amassed an impressive collection of jobs, responsibilities, hobbies, relationships, and other endeavors. And like a hoarder, we picked up each one with honest intent to do something meaningful with it. But time passes, and before we know it

> *"It's then that we discover the truth; that our whole life has become a support system for this hodgepodge of projects and responsibilities. we've amassed."*

we look around and realize we're prisoners of all this garbage strewn about. It's then that we discover the truth; that our whole life has become a support system for this hodgepodge of projects and responsibilities we've amassed. It's time to purge!

RECOGNIZE

One of the reasons we struggle with focusing on what matters is there are real psychological mechanisms skewing our perspective, coaxing us into making what may not be the best decisions. Identifying and recognizing these psychological propensities won't inoculate us against their effects (we understand how the nervous system works, but that doesn't stop us

> **Some of us think holding on makes us strong; but sometimes it is letting go.**
>
> – Hermann Hesse

from screaming to high heaven when we hit our thumb with a hammer), but it will at least help us be less critical of ourselves when we struggle to make the hard elimination decisions.

Sunk Cost

In 1985 my father purchased a 1959 Jaguar Mark I for $1,400. It was in running condition, though a loop around the block was ambitious for the thing. It was in need of a full restoration, which is exactly what my father was interested in doing. And so the process began, and with it, the expenditures. He did a full engine rebuild for around $2,500 and a body alignment, repair, and prime for about $3,000. Along the way he purchased something in the neighborhood of $1,000 worth of parts. Yes, things were going well. But then life took a turn and my father decided to buy and restore a bed and breakfast in Telluride, Colorado. This put the old Jag on pause—a pause that ended up lasting 20 years. Still, he really didn't want to part with the thing. Over the years he had invested thousands of dollars into the venture, countless man-hours, and 20 years' worth of storage fees. After having invested so much in the project, how could he walk away from it? Eventually though he realized that despite all he had invested, he was never going to finish the car, let alone recoup his investment. With a heavy but pragmatic heart, he sold the Mark I on eBay for $350. (And yeah, I totally get the irony as I write these words and look at my MG.)

My father's experience is a good example of how the principle of sunk cost causes us to continue investing in things past the point of no return.[1] It's all about throwing good money after bad. There are many reasons why we do this. Clearly we don't want to be wasteful.[2] We also desperately hold on to the hope that one day we'll be able to recoup our losses. But when it's all said and done, these ships have already sailed.

Another way of looking at how sunk costs affect our decisions is by considering my friend with the timeshare. Some years he has no desire to go to Mazatlán. He'd much rather do something else. But he has already paid for the darn thing so he has no choice, right? I mean, it's either go or flush all those timeshare fees down the drain. But here's the thing: whether he goes or not has nothing to do with the money he has already paid. If he goes; if he doesn't; it doesn't change the fact that the cost is sunk. If he can get greater joy out of going somewhere else that year then why not? But let's say he can't stand the idea of wasting that money so he goes anyway. He still needs to pay transportation, food, additional fees, and so on. He's throwing good money after bad. Still he goes, spends more money, and is miserable the whole time. But hey, at least he didn't waste his money, right?

How often have we hung onto a career track, not because it still gave us a sense of fulfillment, but because we couldn't stand the idea of walking away from all we have invested in climbing the ladder? A good friend of mine is a medical doctor. The man is scary smart and utterly charming to an intimidating degree. You can't help but feel weirdly mortal standing next to this guy. Yet he once confided in me that he was miserable in his job, that if he were honest, he wasn't sure he ever derived any real joy from his chosen vocation. I asked him why he didn't transition to something else. The idea struck him as absurd. After investing so much time, effort, and money in medical school, the idea of leaving all that behind wasn't even in the realm of possibility. His devotion to his sunk costs was greater than his desire to be in a rewarding career.

Opportunity Cost

Shane Frederick of Yale's School of Marketing gives the following example of opportunity cost.

> "While shopping for my first stereo, I spent an hour debating between a $1,000 Pioneer and a $700 Sony. Perhaps fearing that my indecision would cost him a sale, the salesman intervened with the comment 'Well, think of it this way—would you rather have the Pioneer, or the Sony and $300 worth of CDs?'"[3]

That day a Sony and an arm-full of CDs found a new home.

Every time we invest in one thing, we lose the opportunity to invest in another. If I want to go out with my wife but only have $40 then we have some options:

we can hit the bookstore, catch a movie, or have an inexpensive dinner at a greasy spoon. All are right up our alley, so a wonderful evening will be had. However, because our funds are limited, we can't do more than one of these activities. If we choose the bookstore and buy a couple books (a cosmically-decreed inevitability) then we can't go to the movies or grab a bite to eat. Going to the bookstore has *cost* us these opportunities.

In our attempt to "have it all" we often forget to think about what we're forgoing by investing in everything that comes along.[4] For example, in his speech before the American Society of Newspaper Editors entitled *The Chance for Peace*, President Eisenhower put forth the following proposition:

> *"The cost of one modern heavy bomber is this: a modern brick school in more than 30 cities. It is two electric power plants, each serving a town of 60,000 population. It is two fine, fully equipped hospitals. It is some 50 miles of concrete highway. We pay for a single fighter plane with a half million bushels of wheat. We pay for a single destroyer with new homes that could have housed more than 8,000 people."[5]*

Opportunity cost is often cited as a contributor to indecision. We're afraid to fully commit our resources to one opportunity for fear that a better one may come along. This results in one of two things: either we procrastinate the decision until the opportunity passes us by, or we commit to every opportunity that comes along and place them all on sort of a saline drip. This behavior prevents us from fully committing our finite resources to what really matters. Instead, we sprinkle our time, money, and attention across multiple priorities, but not in any quantity that would enable success.

Endowment Effect

Over the last 25 years I've participated in any number of runs, bike centuries, and triathlons; everything from small sprints to full-on Ironman events. And there, tucked away in every athlete swag bag, was the ubiquitous t-shirt, the currency of amateur sports. A t-shirt for this, a t-shirt for that; t-shirts here, there, and everywhere. Some were downright hideous, but most I wore with pride. They were the tangible evidence of something that gave me joy and a sense of accomplishment. Problem is, today some of these shirts are really, *really* old. They're tattered and frayed; faded and stained. In some cases they can't be warn outside the house in good taste (though now and again I sneak one on when my wife isn't paying attention). What's more, I'm running out of places to keep them, to shove them away to make room for my big boy clothes. We're talking dozens and dozens of these old rags, taking up my limited drawer space and never seeing the light of day. So why not cull the herd? Toss a few of them out? Are you nuts?! These are my *t-shirts*! And yet the weird thing is had

I not earned the shirt in a race I wouldn't have paid a nickel for the thing, even to use it as a shop rag. The reason for this is the *endowment effect*.

The endowment effect causes us to ascribe value to things simply because we own them.[6] The problem is, some things we own require resources to maintain. It goes back to the irony of wealth we discussed earlier. Most of our

> *"Just as the useless old t-shirts taking up limited space in my drawers need to be thrown out, so also must we toss out the old activities that have lost their meaning yet take up valuable resources."*

possessions require continued investment to keep them in optimum condition. Cars have to be serviced, yards have to be groomed, homes have to be mended, and clothes have to be stored. But it's more than that. Social media accounts have to be fed, favorite TV series have to be watched, and blogs have to be read. Finally it hits a crescendo. Hobbies have to be sustained, despite the fact they no longer deliver pleasure. Careers have to be built because that's what we've always done.

Just as the useless old t-shirts taking up limited space in my drawers need to be thrown out, so also must we toss out the old activities that have lost their meaning yet take up valuable resources. When this is the case it's up to us to make the hard decisions.

Status Quo Bias

As I mentioned earlier, I've participated in countless sporting events. All required a significant investment of time, money, and energy. Training alone takes up something in the neighborhood of between 400 to 600 hours a year, or around eight to eleven hours a week. Now that may not sound like much, but trust me, it is. What's more, these numbers don't include prep and recovery time, the cognitive resources necessary to stay focused and motivated, eat right, keep from getting sick, juggle schedules, maintain equipment, and so forth. In the end it's a huge resource sink. But here's the thing: since I had done it every year, it became a legacy activity—a shoe-in each time I sat down to make my plans for the following year. It had always been there, and somehow, I figured, it always would be. It had reached the level of *status quo*. But then one year I realized something: participating in another monster event wasn't as important this time around as it had been in the past. Yet making the decision not to sign up for another event was one of the toughest decisions I had to make that year. Not because signing up for a race was important to me, but because I had always fed this hobby in the past and so I felt I needed to keep feeding it in perpetuity, even though the alure had faded.

We have a strong tendency to maintain the status quo, mostly because the disadvantages of changing seem larger than the advantages.[7] But if we're going to perform with intent the status quo has to change.

In Summary

1. **Let go of sunk cost:** Stop throwing good money (and time, energy, resources, etc.) after bad. Declare the patient dead and move on.

2. **Let go of opportunity cost:** You can't have it all, but you can have what matters—and that's all that matters.

3. **Let go of the endowment effect:** Just because in the past you were committed to something doesn't mean you're obligated to always invest in it.

4. **Let go of status quo bias:** If you don't know why you do something any longer, stop.

Your Turn

Let's take a moment to recognize those things that may be unnecessarily siphoning off your finite resources or distracting you from what really matters. That's right; time to pull out the notebook, tablet, or laptop and start jotting down your thoughts. Here are some questions you might consider:

▶ Are there sunk costs out there shackling you to projects or goals that no longer have any particular meaning to you? What investments of time, money, and energy have you made that you're hesitant to walk away from?

_____

_____

_____

_____

_____

_____

_____

▶ What opportunities do you see or anticipate that make it difficult for you to fully commit to performing with intent? Are they really so likely to come to pass or full of promise that they're worth holding back today for the possibility of tomorrow?

_____

_____

_____

_____

_____

_____

_____

▶ What projects, habits, or rituals take up space in your life? Are they providing sufficient return for the investments you make, or can you use these resources for greater effect?

_____

_____

_____

_____

_____

_____

_____

_____

▶ What are you doing today because you've always done it; not because you still get rich reward from the investment of time, energy, and resources?

_____

_____

_____

_____

_____

_____

_____

Like the frog floating in a pot of water sitting on the stove, we don't always recognize that the water is slowly getting hotter and hotter—not until it's too late. Let's figure out where the hotspots are so we can start cooling them down!

RESIGN

It's one thing to recognize the psychological mechanisms that cause us to hang on to the worthless at the expense of the valuable, but it's something else entirely to then act upon this understanding. Acting means making hard choices and sacrificing things that may seem important but don't make the cut. As we do this, many feelings are bound to arise:

You're Going to Miss Out

Earlier we talked about the fear of missing out, or FOMO. We've been conditioned to view opportunities as exciting, desirable, profitable, and worth our while. The word itself, *opportunity*, conjures images of new beginnings, exhilarating days ahead, and happy-ever-afters. As Priya Parker puts it, "We've been taught to relentlessly maximize our options. We live in fear to make sure that we're trying to live the best of our possible future scenarios."[1] It's no wonder then that we find it difficult to turn our back on something that could potentially deliver such promise. Our fear of missing out drives us to set an eager *yes* as our default response when opportunity comes a-knocking.

> **Human progress is neither automatic nor inevitable. ...Every step toward the goal of justice requires sacrifice, suffering, and struggle; the tireless exertions and passionate concern of dedicated individuals.**
>
> *– Martin Luther King, Jr.*

The problem is that FOMO makes us poor discerners of opportunity. We don't always pause to evaluate the cost of investing in an opportunity, the likely rate of return, or even if it really matters to us as much as our other obligations, commitments, and priorities. We chase after everything that comes along, and in so doing put lousy opportunities on par with stellar ones. This is no good, and it has to stop.

It goes without saying that we can't simply flip a switch and get over our fear of missing out. It takes work and discipline. However, the results can be indescribably liberating. No longer shackled to the need to chase every opportunity as though our lives depended on it, we can free ourselves to fully invest in what really matters, free of guilt and anxiety. Here are a few ways we can begin to free ourselves of the fear of missing out:

▶ Focus on purpose, productivity, and being busy—in that order. If what we're working on supports what's important—which is to say it has purpose and meaning to us—then great. That's first. Next we should make sure everything we do supports that purpose and moves the ball down the field—is productive. Excellent. Then—and only then—can we get our busy addition fix. Remember, it's not about getting things done, it's getting the *right* things done for the *right purpose.*

▶ Accept that yes, we're going to miss out on some things. Get over it. In missing out on some things we're investing more time and effort into other things—things that matter. We can't be everywhere, doing everything, all the time. Realize that we'll never win the FOMO battle, so why fight it?

▶ Remember the law of opportunity cost: every time we say *yes* to an opportunity we're reducing the resources we can invest in achieving our goals. In other words, a *yes* in one area may mean failure in another.

▶ Block out the distractions. Unplug. Schedule and limit time spent online. Get rid of all that nonsense that sucks time away. Silence the cell phone. Turn off the notification function. Seriously. I'm forever astonished by how many people have their phones on in movies, lectures, meetings, classrooms, and so forth. Silence it and put it away.

▶ Take a walk (and leave the phone at home). We should intentionally disconnect and allow our minds to be alone with their thoughts, questions, hopes, and ambitions. That gooey organ between our ears is pretty darn smart. Turn off the external static of life and let it do its thing. TV, radio, emails, texts, phone calls, meetings, Twitter, Facebook, Instagram, Snapchat, LinkedIn, YouTube—all these things would like us to think that they're helping us gather and synthesize information, but more often than not they're doing just the opposite. They can fill our heads with white noise and prevent us from honing our laser-sharp intellect and passions in on what really matters.

You're Going to Lose Something

We've invested time, energy, money; and in some cases blood, sweat, and tears into projects that now, in the cool harsh light of day, don't really matter. It's time to cut these things loose and move on. Yes, this means we'll be walking away from everything we've built and invested, but remember, we'll be walking away from something that doesn't matter and walking toward something that does. Think of it this way: would you pay to get out of a contract that wasn't generating any return so that you could close that chapter and instead invest your resources in something that had a much greater rate of return? I would. I'm not saying it would be easy. I'd still have to swallow hard before walking away from all I had invested, but if the plant is dead, why keep watering it? Better to cut our losses and turn our focused attention to more promising prospects.

You're Going to Feel like a Failure

There's no way to sugar coat this. Walking away from something that isn't working is going to feel like failure. And you know what? Maybe it is. But that's okay. Later we'll learn more about how to learn from our failures, but that won't change the fact that falling short of a goal stings our pride. But it has to be done. So yes, sure, we quit before reaching our goals. But which would you rather do: make the conscience decision to shift your finite resources to something with greater potential, or continue investing anemic levels of resources into something that'll do nothing but wither on the vine? Quit now, while you still have something to invest, or fail later, after having lost everything. It'll take courage and humility, but in the end the things that really matter will benefit.

Just Because You Can Do It Yourself Doesn't Mean You Should Do It Yourself

A friend of mine spent years handling the books and maintaining the website for her consulting firm. It was a source of great frustration for her. The accounting side was simple enough, but numbers weren't her thing. As a result she often procrastinated the task until she couldn't put it off any longer. But as much as she disliked doing the accounting, it was nothing compared to maintaining her company website. She had no training, very little in the way of technical inclination, and nothing to speak of in terms of understanding user experience. Then there was creating content, keeping the articles and pages fresh and new. And forget trying to keep up with the latest technology and operating systems! She was in over her head, but what's worse, every hour she spent wrangling the finances and website was an hour she wasn't earning. Now the obvious thing to do would be to outsource this. She knew this, but she couldn't shake the idea that it would be a waste of money. "It's not so hard," she'd tell herself. "Why should I pay someone to do this when I've been managing for years now?" Eventually though she came around and sent these things out to be done by experts. No longer did she worry about the accounting and the website. Instead she spent more time doing what she loved—taking care of her clients. In the end the added business more than made up for the cost of outsourcing these administrative tasks.

Some things have to be done. That's what our obligations and commitments are all about. However, there's nothing that says *we* have to do them. There are others more capable, more expert, and more efficient in doing these things that can help us out. "Yeah, but they cost money," you might say. True. But when we do these things it costs us time, energy, and cognitive resources; and oftentimes these things are more valuable than money. I'm not saying we should outsource everything, but I am saying that every time we decide to do something ourselves versus send it out to be done we're making resource decisions.

In Summary

1. **You're going to miss out:** Accept that yes, you'll miss out on some things. What of it? In missing out on things that don't matter you're investing more time and effort into things that do matter.

2. **You're going to lose something:** Yes, you'll lose something—of lesser value—and in so doing you'll gain something of tremendous value.

3. **You're going to feel like a failure:** That's right. You'll join the ranks of Albert Einstein who walked away from an unremarkable career as a patent clerk, or Walt Disney who was fired as a journalist for having a lack of imagination and no original ideas. I'm only guessing here, but I doubt either one of these icons felt like failures for too terribly long.

4. **Just because you can do it yourself doesn't mean you should do it yourself:** You're only successful when you intelligently allocate your limited resources. This may mean asking someone else do something you're used to doing yourself.

Your Turn

Few of the steps involved in the ADEPT Model are easy, and this phase is certainly no exception. But if you're going to accomplish truly incredible and meaningful things you need to heave the deadweight over the rails. So ask yourself these questions:

▶   What do you fear giving up the most?

_____

_____

_____

_____

_____

_____

_____

_____

▶   What are you afraid you'll miss out on if you turn away from something?

_____

_____

_____

_____

_____

_____

_____

▶ Are their people in your life that'll wonder why you've given up on something you said you were going to do? What do you plan on telling these supporters?

_____

_____

_____

_____

_____

_____

_____

_____

By making the tough decisions now you're going to set yourself up for greater success tomorrow.

TAKE CHARGE

The other day I saw a small notebook in a consignment shop with a cover that made me smile:

"Don't put off 'til tomorrow what you can straight up cancel."

> **The things which are most important don't always scream the loudest.**
>
> – Bob Hawke

I couldn't have put it better myself.

Now that we recognize the psychological mechanisms that prevent us from performing with intent, and have resigned ourselves to the fact that this process is going to come with no small amount of discomfort, we're ready to gird up our loins and take charge. This means doing the following five things:

► Eliminate distractions.

► Beware of scope creep.

► Don't make a career out of a task.

► Beware of bring-me-a-rock exercises.

► Beware of the foot-in-the-door effect.

Let's explore each one of these in detail.

1. Eliminate Distractions

Oh how we love distractions!

Distractions provide a way for us to interact with others and feed our need for human connection.[1] They give us a respite from the drudgery of the task.[2] They can help stimulate our flagging attention, giving our minds something else to think about for a moment before turning their attention back to the task at hand.[3,4] What's more, distractions are addictive and can help us feel better.[5]

This is all well and good, except for one important thing: distractions are… well…distracting. They distract us from what matters and waste our limited resources. Performing with intent means eschewing purposeless distractions and focusing on what matters. This doesn't mean we can't decompress now and again, watch some TV, go to a movie, or enjoy some personal time. All work and no play makes Jack a dull boy. (More about that later.) We simply need to make sure these things aren't getting in the way of what needs to be done.

Dan Heath, Senior Fellow at Duke University, understood this when he took draconian measures to remove online distractions. He bought an old laptop and deleted all its browsers and wireless network drivers. Armed with this "way-back machine," Dan would go to the coffee shop or library and be completely isolated from the cacophony of the Internet. As his brother Chip put it, he'd been liberated by this restriction.[6]

So ask yourself, what does your rogues gallery of distraction look like? Who's standing along the wall in that surly lineup? Now's the time to scrutinize these bandits carefully and tell them there's a new sheriff in town. Roust them with extreme prejudice! Here's how:

Say No

As humans, we want to get along, to be helpful, and to be liked. Saying *no* works against this innate drive and so can feel very awkward.[7] Even if we know we should say *no*, saying *yes* feels easier, even if we really have no intention of following through. This isn't good for us, nor is it any good for those asking for our assistance.

Performing with intent means turning away from those things that would distract us from what matters and unnecessarily drain our resources. If the request doesn't fit into what matters, then it doesn't matter. As McKeown says in his book, *Essentialism*, "If it isn't a clear *yes*, then it's a clear *no*."[8] Consider the following:

▶ Everyone wants something from us. Everyone. But only we know how much time, money, and other resources we have available to invest. It's not their job to know. Their job is to try to get us to help them do something; our job is to responsibly budget our resources.

▶ A noncommittal *yes* can do more harm than a clear *no*. Let's say someone asks us to do him a favor. Nothing complicated, maybe a day or two of work, no big deal. We agree, but even as we see the word *yes* float out in front of us we almost regret having agreed. So we sort of do it. A few minutes here, maybe an hour there. A week goes by, then two. Before long a month has gone by and we still haven't made any real headway. In the meantime, our friend, who was counting on us, has put the rest of his project on hold. He's waiting, maybe others are as well. We realize what a mess we've created and start to feel guilty. We avoid phone calls. Generally a bad situation. On the other hand, had we said *no* in the first place our friend would have been able to move on and find someone who could deliver what he needed. No harm done. Sure, he might be disappointed that we didn't agree to help, but this is much less damaging than broken trust.

▶ Every time we say *no* to something less important we're saying *yes* to things that really matter. Saying *no* isn't a selfish act; it's a reaffirmation of a good decision already made.

How to Say No

If saying *no* were easy we wouldn't be having this conversation. While I can't completely remove the awkward feeling that accompanies rejection, there are a few things we can do make it a little easier:

▶ Say *no*, I mean the actual word: *No*. Obvious, right? The problem is we don't often say *no*. Instead we say things like, "I'm busy this week" or "I would but I have another commitment." On the surface these responses may seem fine enough, but while they close the front door, they can inadvertently open a back window. "How about next week?" the person might ask, or, "How about if you get it started and I'll pick it back up when you run out of time?" This places us in a difficult position. Now if we say *no* we'll come across as inflexible, not open to negotiation or compromise. The asker is clearly being reasonable and respectful of our time. Maybe we can help a little, right? The road to hell, my friends. The road to hell. Had we said *no* in the first place the boundaries would have been set. This isn't to say the requestor won't take another run at us, but at least this time we won't come across as being slippery by holding our ground. By saying *no* the first time we're not changing our tune when we continue to resist and stick to our guns.

▶ Beware of the *follow-up*. The other day a not-for-profit organization I support called and asked if I'd be willing to double my monthly sustaining contribution. *Willing*? Yes. *Able*? No, sorry. My budget was tight so I had to decline. But my caller continued. Would I be willing to increase my contribution by a few dollars? Well sure, I guess I can do that. What's another $30 or so a year? Welcome to the *follow-up*. In this particular instance I was fine with the outcome, but it taught me an important lesson. What asker would be worth his salt if he didn't try to break down our defenses? The second ask is often accompanied by compromise and negotiation. An initial ask for one day may be followed-up with a request for a few hours.

Can't donate $100? How about $50? Surely you can afford a few hours and a couple dollars? See what I mean?

▶ Be brief and succinct. State your case and move on. Don't over-explain. Over-explaining opens those back windows we were talking about and leaves us vulnerable to countermoves. Worse still, we may find ourselves talking ourselves into a *yes!* Pack that nonsense away and respectfully decline the request.

▶ When appropriate, follow up the *no* with a, "But this is what I can do." It may be what the person is asking for is really more than is needed. Or maybe we have something at our fingertips that can meet the spirit of the request. One time a friend asked me if I could write an education reimbursement policy for his company. I said no, but what I could do was pull down some boilerplate examples and templates for the members-only resources section of a website I had access to. In the end this more than met my friend's need, and all it cost me was a few minutes.

▶ If the person is someone in authority and is insistent, ask what he or she would like you to de-prioritize. Most the time when people ask us to do something the cost of the request isn't calculated. By making it clear that the request comes with a price we place value on our time and effort. It's then up to the requestor to decide what's most important and pay the price on the label. Remind the world that there's no such thing as a free lunch.[9]

▶ On a related note, get rid of guilt piles. What are guilt piles? Well, see that stack of books we keep telling ourselves we're going to read but know we won't? That list of blogs we've bookmarked for later? Those saved emails with articles from friends and coworkers that we've put off for months? These are all examples of guilt piles: things that do nothing more than remind us on a daily basis of the broken promises we've made to ourselves and others. Ditch them. Give the books back to you friends, delete the bookmarks and emails, and release yourself from the shackles of self-imposed guilt and shame.

2. Beware of Scope Creep

The Bradley Fighting Vehicle was originally developed as an armored personnel carrier, designed to hold eleven troops and move quickly through a combat zone. However, the various fighting forces wanted to use this vehicle as well, but to do so they needed their unique requirements met. With that entered the evils of *scope creep*. Scope creep is when continuous and uncontrolled changes work their way into a plan. Over the course of several years the vehicle was transformed into a hybrid of a troop carrier, scout vehicle, and anti-tank weapons platform. To make room for the technology, weaponry, and munitions, the troop compliment was reduced from eleven to six. It was also constructed of lightweight aluminum to be fast enough to serve as a scout vehicle. This, despite the fact that it had enough firepower to rival many tanks. The aluminum armor was much too weak to withstand a strike from a typical Soviet anti-tank weapon, much less a shot from an enemy tank. What was finally put into production over a decade later, as the satirical film *The Pentagon Wars* put it, was, "A troop transport that can't carry troops, a reconnaissance vehicle that's too conspicuous to do reconnaissance, and a quasi-tank that has less armor than a snow blower, but has enough ammo to take out half of D.C."[10]

What makes scope creep so insidious is it builds itself upon a series of steps that, when examined in isolation, are perfectly reasonable and even defensible. However, bit by bit, these steps take us to a place far from where we started. For example, some time back I was an HR manager for a small technology company. One of my responsibilities was employee training, which made good sense. Employee development clearly falls within the prevue of HR, and I was happy to own that responsibility. Then one day my director said he'd like me to do some of the customer training as well. Same topics, same material, only a different audience. Sure, I guess I can do that. I mean, I already have all the training modules pulled together. So what if I'm training customers as well as employees? It's all the same to me, right? A few months pass. My director asks me to deliver new product training to customers as well, training designed to give our more top-shelf customers a sneak peek at what's coming down the pike. I'm going to have to develop training for these products anyway, he explains, so getting me in on rollout would make it easier down the line. Okay, I say, though now I'm getting nervous. I mean, sure, I guess it makes sense to be on the forefront, since ultimately I'm responsible for internal and external training. It's all good, right? A month goes by. Hey Lon, I'd like you to help Marketing put together some new product material. Since you're doing all the new product training and are close to the customers, you have a good idea what'll resonate with them and what won't. You have to develop material for your training anyway, so we might as well get more mileage out of this content and use it for marketing as well as training. Now that I think about it, says my director, what do you think about merging Marketing with HR?

See what I mean? Look at any one of these steps and the argument can be made. But look at the beginning and the end and you have an HR manager leading the marketing department. This, my friends, is classic scope creep.

3. Don't Make a Career Out of a Task

One early morning during the nightshift at the FedEx hub in Memphis I was taping up a box that had begun to work its way open. I must have been pretty exuberant with the tape gun because after a couple minutes one of the ramp agents came over and said, "Hey Lon, don't make a career out of that box." He was right. The box was taped just fine. Our customer's shipment was secure and it was time to move it on to the next phase of its journey—getting it on that plane on time!

There's a job to be done, but after that there's another job to be done. And after that another. There will always be work to be done, so don't fixate on a task and make it into something bigger than it really is. Get it done and move on. I'm not saying we should do shoddy work. Do it and do it right. What I am saying though is eventually the law of depreciating return kicks in and we're no longer getting sufficient value for the amount of time and resources we're dedicating to a task.

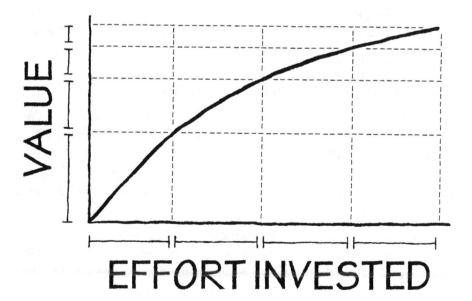

4. Beware of Bring-Me-a-Rock Exercises

A man tells another to bring him a rock.

"Okay, here's a rock," says the second man.

"No, not that rock. A different rock."

"All right. Here's a different rock."

"No, no, you're not hearing me," the first man says. "I don't want that kind of rock. I want a different rock."

"How about if you tell me exactly what kind of rock you want me to bring," the second man says.

"What do you mean, 'what kind of rock?' A rock! Hard, Cold. You know, like these here but not so…I don't know…just not so. Why is this so difficult for you to understand?"

Sound familiar?

As we discussed earlier, there are any number of people with claim on our time and resources, and that's fine. It's called life. But what isn't fine is when these claims are nebulous and poorly defined. Things require our time and attention, but no more than is necessary to meet the need. If we start to feel ourselves being pulled into a *bring-me-a-rock exercise*, we should call timeout, zero in on the expectations, figure out what exactly needs to be done by when and by whom, do it, then move on.

5. Beware of the Foot-in-the-Door Effect

The *foot-in-the-door effect* happens when someone gets us to agree to a small request, then advances a related but larger request. You see, since we've agreed to the first request, we're more inclined to agree to the second, larger request. By saying *yes* the first time we established ourselves as helpful and flexible, a pleasant self-image. We want to maintain this image and so feel a pull to agreeing to the larger request.[11]

When we sense a foot-in-the-door scenario may be afoot (I crack me up!), we need to pause and ask the person making the initial request what may possibly be asked of us once we're done. I once had a student ask if I'd be willing to take a look at his paper before submitting it, just to make sure he was on the right track. It seemed a reasonable enough of a request, so I said sure, send it along. I took a look at it, saw that he was on his way to delivering a fine paper, and sent him an email to that effect. He then wrote back and asked if I wouldn't mind providing specific feedback on certain sections and give it an overall critique. I struggled with this. I wanted to say, "Sure." On the other hand, what he was basically asking me to do was to help him write his paper. I had fallen prey to the foot-in-the-door effect. Begrudgingly I agreed. But then a couple weeks later he did it again, asking for me if I'd take a look at his paper and tell him if he was on the right track. This time I was more prepared. I asked if he was formally submitting the paper to be graded. He said no, to which I said that I'd then be happy to tell him if he was missing any marks, but that I wouldn't be doing a complete review of the paper. At first he was a little taken aback, but he understood my position and agreed. I had this student for two more courses, and our agreement stood fast for the remainder of our time together.

In Summary

1. **Eliminate distractions:** Distractions seduce you away from what matters and waste your limited resources. Performing with intent means eschewing distractions and focusing on what matters.

2. **Say *no*:** Every time you say *no* to something less important you're saying *yes* to something more important. Saying *no* isn't a selfish act; it's a reaffirmation of a good decision already made.

3. **Beware of scope creep:** Scope creep slowly and carefully leads you from the path and into the woods, away from what matters and toward mediocrity.

4. **Beware of bring-me-a-rock exercises:** Things require your time and attention, but no more than is necessary to meet the need. If you start to feel yourself being pulled into a bring-me-a-rock exercise, call timeout, zero in on the expectations, do it, then move on.

5. **Beware of the foot-in-the-door effect:** If you sense that a foot-in-the-door scenario may be taking place, ask the person what may possibly be asked of you once you've done as requested.

Your Turn

Taking charge often means taking charge from those who had claim to your resources in the past. These masters—whether electronic or flesh-and-blood—will resist and do everything within their power to suck you back in. The better you identify these masters and the power they hold over you, the better you'll be able to resist their call. With that as context, think about the following:

▶ Make a list of things that distract you from performing with intent. Is it surfing social media? Watching TV? Reading fluff books? We all have our guilty pleasures, and in small doses they don't pose a problem, but do any get away from you?

_____

_____

_____

_____

_____

_____

_____

▶ Do you find it difficult to say *no*? If so, why do you think this is? Are you afraid it will damage a relationship? Do you feel you owe the person? Do you like being the "go-to" person—someone others can rely on to help get things done?

_____

_____

_____

_____

_____

_____

_____

► Is scope creep a problem for you? If so, why? Maybe you're very good at seeing how everything is interconnected and so have a hard time delineating a project's boundaries. A good friend of mine has this superpower: the ability to see all the connection points in the universe. As a result he struggles with keeping things out of scope. On the other hand, maybe it's connected with your difficulty in saying *no*. Scope creep will be a way of life if every time a request comes in the answer is *yes*. Maybe you feel it's your job to do as you're asked (or told) so you may feel that fighting scope creep isn't really an option. Is that truly the case?

_____

_____

_____

_____

_____

_____

_____

_____

► Do you often find yourself running in circles in a never-ending bring-me-a-rock exercise? What has this cost you in the past? What are ways you can combat it in the future?

_____

_____

_____

_____

_____

_____

_____

_____

► Have you ever fallen for the foot-in-the-door approach? What can you do
  to prevent this the next time it comes around?

_____

_____

_____

_____

_____

_____

_____

_____

Remember, the better you understand those who would own you, the better
you'll be able to manager them and take the power for yourself!

ELIMINATE AND PRIORITIZE

I once worked with someone who really struggled to prioritize tasks and objectives. There was always far more on his plate than any one person could ever hope to accomplish in the time allotted, but he couldn't see this. When I would tell him we only had two

If you chase two rabbits, you will not catch either one.

– Russian Proverb

weeks left before the CEO would want to see what we had accomplished, so which of the 87 things on the list were the most important to the company, he would inevitably say, "They're all important." I believe in his mind ranking everything as equally important was a matter of principle. He felt they were all interconnected and so if we didn't deliver one then we couldn't deliver on any. There's something admirable and big-picture to this way of thinking, but it's also tragically flawed. As Lencioni says, "If everything is important then nothing is."[1] I wasn't asking my coworker which tasks and objectives were unimportant and therefore a candidate for elimination; I was asking him how we should sequence the tasks so we could start knocking them out and make progress. Unfortunately for him it was an all-or-nothing proposition. As a result, I'm sorry to say, it came down on the nothing side.

Paradoxically, prioritizing allows us to accomplish more than if we were to assign equal value to everything. Consider the analogy of the big rocks offered by Stephen Covey in his book, *First Things First.*[2]

Imagine a glass mason jar, large enough to hold a gallon or so. The space in this jar represents our life—our time, energy, cognitive resources—everything we bring to the table to accomplish a goal. How we fill this jar is determined by how we allocate our finite resources.

Now, many of us spend part of our day doing things that have little value, things like browsing social media, surfing the Internet, watching TV, and so on. To represent the time we spend on nonsense like this we partially fill the jar with water. Not a lot; a fifth or so.

Great, we say. We've lollygagged the morning away, but now it's time to get to work. So we check our email, make phone calls, and read articles. We represent this by adding sand to the jar. These are small busy activities that—in relation to what really matters—aren't that important. We do them for all the reasons we discussed earlier: to eschew the perception of being idle, to hide from our larger responsibilities, and because we just plain like feeling busy.

By this time the jar is about half full, but we really need to get some actual work done today, so we add gravel. Now we're filling out forms, compiling reports, running errands, and holding meetings with coworkers, teachers, and so on. Meetings—lots and lots of meetings.

Now the jar is all but full, and yet we really haven't moved the ball down the field in terms of what matters most—our big rocks. We realize that while we've been "super busy" all day, we haven't been very productive when it comes to the big important things. So we try to fit the big rocks into the jar. But guess what? There's no room. By piddling the day away on the little things we've run out of time and resources to pay attention to what really matters.

But now here's the thing: had we prioritized the big rocks first, we would have been able to do everything that before we were unable to complete. Had we started with the big rocks, then moved on to the gravel, then the sand and even the water, everything would have fit in the jar nicely.

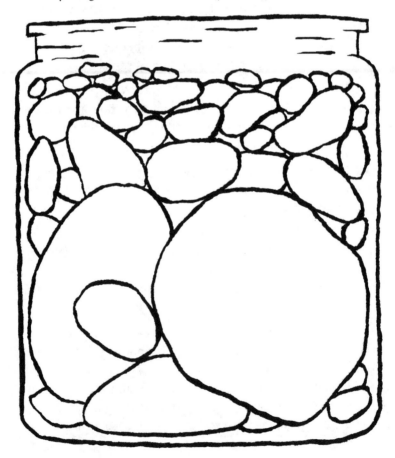

"Achievers always work from a clear sense of priority,"[3] says Gary Keller, cofounder of Keller William Realty, and he's right. By prioritizing what matters we're able to accomplish far more than if we run about, saying everything is equally important.

In Summary

1. **Achievers always work from a clear sense of priority:** If everything is important then nothing is.

Your Turn

You already know you can't do everything, so it's time to decide what gets done and what gets dumped. It's time to "kill your darlings," so to speak, and eliminate what takes up your time but doesn't matter (as much). To this end, refer back to your list of spinning plates (the demands you have in your time and resources) and the thoughts you wrote down as you went through this chapter. See what can be eliminated. To move through this filtration process, do the following:

▶ Write down specifically what you're going to eliminate (projects, hobbies, recreations, jobs, responsibilities etc.).

_____

_____

_____

_____

_____

_____

_____

_____

▶ What do you need to do to put an end to these activities?

_____

_____

_____

_____

_____

_____

_____

▶ Who are the supporters of these activities? How do you plan to discuss your decision to eliminate these things?

_____

_____

_____

_____

_____

_____

_____

_____

▶ How will the elimination of these activities affect your relationships?

_____

_____

_____

_____

_____

_____

_____

_____

I know; this is hard. *Really* hard. But this is what has to be done. Think of it as moving out of your 2,000-square-foot home into a 140-foot tiny house. There's not enough room for everything, so it's time to jettison the clutter.

As you work through this difficult process, remember how much you'll be freeing yourself up for those things that matter in your life. Tell those close to you why you're doing this. My guess is they'll support you gladly. Still, there are things we can do to help make this happen. More about this later.

CHAPTER 6: PLAN
(what matters)

Being busy does not always mean real work. The object of all work is production or accomplishment and to either of these ends there must be forethought, system, planning, intelligence, and honest purpose, as well as perspiration. Seeming to do is not doing.

– Thomas A. Edison
American inventor, businessman

Now that we understand the economic laws of performing with intent, have discovered what really matters, and have eliminated what doesn't matter, all that's left is to get out there and seize the day! Okay, but how? How do we muster our resources in such a way as to be laser-focused on the objective, getting all the wood behind the arrow? Step by step and brick by brick. And to do this, we need a plan.

There's an ancient legend that offers a marvelous lesson in the virtues of planning. One day the designer of the Jiayuguan pass in the Great Wall of China was visited by the officer in charge of materials. The officer asked the designer how many bricks he would need to build the pass. Well this designer was no slouch and apparently knew his way around an abacus, because he replied with a weirdly specific number: 99,999. The officer in change asked how much buffer was built in that number—extra bricks to account a missed calculation here or a slipup there. The designer said none. He needed exactly 99,999 bricks. The materials officer was dubious. This wasn't his first rodeo either. He commanded his charge to order extra bricks, just in case. The designer bristled at the notion but knew on which side his bread was buttered, so he did as he was directed and ordered an extra brick—*one* brick. When the Jiayuguan pass was completed there it was; one extra brick. To tout his perfect planning, his men placed the loose brick on an overhang where it remains to this day; a tangible symbol of perfect planning.

Sometimes when we look at a massive objective—building a career, earning a degree, raising a family, writing a book, remodeling a home, you name it—it's easy to get overwhelmed by the sheer enormity of it all. Where do we start? Projects such as these start with a big picture then work themselves down to specific daily tasks. That's exactly what we're going to do—with *Planning*.

Of all the elements of the ADEPT Model, *Planning* is perhaps my favorite. In fact, it may be that I like planning *too* much. I can spend hours—even days or weeks—planning something far past the point necessary to get my ducks in a row. Maybe it speaks to my need for control, or it could be that it's the first step in the model that lets us finally get to work—to actually feel like we're starting our journey, not just thinking about it. It could also be that I've experienced the incredible highs of (as Hannibal of the *A-Team* might say) seeing a plan come together, as well as the devastating lows of missing the mark because I didn't plan enough. Whatever the reason, I sincerely hope I can persuade you of the incredible rewards waiting for you on the other side of a solid plan. So with that, let's get started.

THE BENEFITS OF PLANNING

Planning is a vital part of the ADEPT Model, yet when I teach planning to my college students, inevitably someone will ask whether all of this is really necessary. It may sound like an impetuous question, but it's one that has spurred a great deal of debate in the business and entrepreneur community. Having taken the time to decide what really matters and eliminate the superfluous distractions, we may be raring to hit the ground running, damn the torpedoes, full steam ahead. But while this is understandable, let me assure you, planning pays off.[1] Always. And in spades. It shouldn't be that hard to grasp. No one ever launched a satellite, built a skyscraper, developed a vaccine, invented a new technology, won a championship, or performed life-saving surgery without a plan. Are your endeavors any less important? Let me go ahead and answer that for you: no—your projects matter. If it's worth doing it's worth doing right, and that means doing it with a plan.

By planning we'll be able to:

▶ Stay on target.

▶ See progress.

▶ Intelligently allocate resources.

▶ Determine what works and what doesn't.

▶ Stay motivated.

▶ Anticipate obstacles.

▶ Save time.

▶ Enable faster decision-making.

▶ Increase the likelihood of success.

These are no small promises. As we'll discuss later, life has this incredible way of throwing curve balls at us whenever we try to hunker down and do something important. Working with purposeful intent takes hard work and discipline—things that are difficult to sustain for any length of time. Without a solid plan it's easy to jump the rails when things get tough. Plans give us the structure and momentum we need to plow through the challenges set before us and reach our final destination. So with this in mind, let's look at how we can use planning discipline to perform with intent.

MAPPING THE JOURNEY

For as long as we can remember, maps have shown us how to get where we want to go, the obstacles that await us along the journey, and the places where we can rest and resupply along the way. Maps have been described as "controlled abstractions,"[1] which is a great description of the purpose we need our map to serve. By the time we're done, our map will bring concrete structure to what can be very abstract concepts—concepts such as meaning and purpose.

> **He, who every morning plans the transactions of the day, and follows that plan, carries a thread that will guide him through a labyrinth of the most busy life.**
>
> *– Victor Hugo*

Making Big Things Small; Complex Things Simple

Mark Twain once said, "The secret of getting ahead is getting started. The secret to getting started is breaking your complex, overwhelming tasks into small, manageable tasks, and then starting on the first one." In his book, *The ONE Thing*, Gary Keller maps this idea out in a clear and simple steps.[2] He asks, what is something you want to accomplish in a year? With this in mind, what are you going to do this month? This week? This day? And finally, right now, at this very moment? Our map is going to follow a similar vein, directing our efforts purposefully toward our goals. To do all this we'll map out our:

1. **North Star:** Why we do what we do.

2. **Path:** How we do what we do.

3. **Destination:** Where we're going in the long-term.

4. **Milestones:** Where we're going in the short-term.

5. **Steps:** What we're going to do right now to make it all happen.

1. Your North Star – Your Why

Before we embark on any journey we need to know where we're going and why. Charles Darwin traveled to the Galapagos Islands to engage in scientific research. Lewis and Clark traveled west to blaze a trail for future expansion of the new American nation. The United States went to the moon to establish itself as the leader in the space race. It's not enough to simply know where we want to go. Not by a long shot. The *why* is the most important element of our journey. Without a *why*, our expedition will crumble at the first signs of unfavorable winds and stormy seas. The *why* is what allows us to muster the courage necessary and persevere when those without purpose would fold their maps and go home.

Our *why* shouldn't be so much an actual goal or destination as a psychological driver and purpose. For Darwin it was scientific research, something that's never "done." The same can be said for expansion of the country or dominance in space exploration. This is important because, as we'll see later, there are any number of ways for us to approach our North Star. Likewise, there will be times when we'll need to be flexible in achieving our objectives. For example, Lewis and Clark's expedition centered on finding an all-water route from the east coast to the Pacific. President Jefferson's instructions to the explores were very clear on this point:

> "The object of your mission is to explore the Missouri River, & such principle stream of it, as, by its course and communication with the waters of the Pacific ocean, whether the Columbia, Oregon, Colorado or any other river may offer the most direct & practicable water communication across this continent for the purpose of commerce."[1]

Well guess what, there *is* no east–to–west water passage! So by the strict definition of success spelled out by Jefferson, the expedition was a failure, right? Not even close. Today the US is what it is thanks in no small part to the work of these two men, their guides, and those who lent their support. Their North Star exists yet today and continues to guide many who would try to bring economic opportunity to others. When a sailor navigates by the northern star, he knows he'll never reach it, but it nonetheless guides his every decision.

How do we determine our *why*? By asking ourselves why, of course! But not once; several times. For example, in root-cause analysis there's something called *The 5 Whys*. It's a way of working an issue down to the underlying problem. By doing this we can focus on the problem and not the symptom. For instance, the kitchen floor is wet:

1.   **Why?** *Because the dishwasher is flooding.*

2.   **Why?** *Because the dishwasher isn't draining.*

3.   **Why?** *Because the drain is clogged.*

4.   **Why?** *Because it's gummed up with grease.*

5.   **Why?** *Because we've been pouring bacon grease down the drain.*

On the surface it may have seemed like the problem was a wet kitchen floor, an easy fix. But as it turns out, that wasn't the problem at all, just a symptom of the underlying root-cause.

We can use the same exercise to help us determine our North Star. For instance, when I ask my college students why they're pursuing a degree, they often tell me it's because they want more money. So that's their North Star, right? Not necessarily. Let's apply *The 5 Whys* and see what we come up with:

1.   **Why do you need a degree?** *"Because I want more money."*

2.   **Why do you want more money?** *"Because I want to provide my family with a comfortable living."*

3.   **Why do you want to provide your family with a comfort?** *"I want to provide my children with the opportunity take music lessons, participate in sports, enroll in art or dance classes—anything they want to try. All this costs money."*

4.   **Why do you want to provide these kinds of opportunities?** *"Because this will help my kids learn to work well with others, appreciate the value of diversity, build strong relationships, and develop an understanding of the human condition."*

5.   **Why do you want your kids to learn these things?** *"Because really, there's nothing more important than raising up the next generation. If I can teach my children to be responsible and moral contributors to society then I've fulfilled my purpose as a parent."*

You see? By following this simple five-step process we find that this college student isn't attending class to earn more money; he's there to enable a better, more fulfilling life for his children. Money is simply a vehicle.

Based on this, we can set the following North Star:

Teach my children to be responsible and moral contributors to society.

Understanding this North Star is incredibly important. When the slings and arrows of outrageous fortune (difficult instructors, tuition fees, boring classes, and heinous assignments) come flying, this student be able to draw strength from his North Star—the *why*. Our college student may find a particular class unbearably tedious or a professor an unmitigated ass, but understanding his larger *why* will help him get through these rough patches. This is what our North Star can do for us.

Now some may say this was a pretty predictable exercise, that the desire to provide for one's family is an obvious conclusion. Not so. Many people earn money for many different reasons. Donald Trump once said, "Money was never a big motivation for me, except as a way to keep score. The real excitement is playing the game."[2] Steve "Woz" Wozniak of Apple said, "My goal wasn't to make a ton of money. It was to build good computers."[3] John D. Rockefeller said, "God gave me my money. I believe the power to make money is a gift from God…to be developed and used to the best of our ability for the good of mankind. Having been endowed with the gift I possess, I believe it is my duty to make money and still more money and to use the money I make for the good of my fellow man according to the dictates of my conscience."[4] Though all of these men were ferociously successful at accumulating wealth, the *why* for each was very different. Think of a young woman working on her medical degree. Is she doing it for the prestige? The earning potential? The chance to help people live better lives? To please her parents? To find a cure for a disease that decimated her family? Understanding her own *why* will help her tough through the years of schooling, the grueling schedules, and the massive student loan payments waiting for her on the other side. All this and more will tax her resolve, but if she's committed to her *why* then she'll weather the storms.

In Summary

1. **Your North Star continually directs you toward your *why*:** Before you embark on any journey you need to know where you're going and why. Your North Star gives you purposeful direction. It sets the tone for the life you want to live.

Your Turn

It's time to discover your North Star—that thing, principle, or objective around which you'll chart your course. As you go about this process, consider the following:

▶ Refer back to your guiding principles and see in what way they point you toward a North Star.

_____

_____

_____

_____

_____

_____

_____

▶ Why do you do what you do? Is it to provide for your family? To become the best at something you can possibly become? To effect meaningful change around some cause? To express something inside you that cannot be contained? To simply live a good and happy life? Remember, there's no right or wrong *why*, so don't get hung up if your *why* doesn't feel grand or noble. All that matters is that it drives you.

_____

_____

_____

_____

_____

_____

▶ If your success were guaranteed—if you knew you couldn't fail—what would to do? Don't rush it; take your time. But with this in mind, ask yourself why? Of all the guaranteed successes you could have possibly chosen, why was this one the most important?

_____

_____

_____

_____

_____

_____

_____

_____

With this light to guide your actions you'll magnify the power and intent of your performance. Remember, it's not about reaching your North Star; it's about letting it guide your course.

2. Your Path – Your How

We have our North Star in hand—the thing, principle, or objective around which we navigate our lives. The question now is, how are we going to strive toward this North Star? That's where our Path comes in. If our North Star is our *why*, our Path is our *how*.

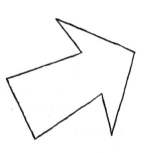

Let's turn back to our college student for a moment and see how this applies to him. His North Star was as follows:

Teach my children to be responsible and moral contributors to society.

This is his *why*—why he does what he does. But it says nothing about how he actually does it. A North Star statement such as this begs the questions of *how*—how is this young man going to live his life in accordance with this North Star? The answer to that question is in the Path he selects.

Again, don't make the mistake of thinking the answer to this question is obvious. There are many ways one can go about raising up a morally and socially responsible generation. Consider the question of how to provide an education for the children:

▶ **Homeschooling rationale:** *"This is the best way for me to instill the guiding principles I feel are necessary to live a morally and socially responsible life."*

▶ **Public education rationale:** *"This is the best way for my children to learn to work with others from all walks of life and be a productive member of a diverse community."*

▶ **Boarding school rationale:** *"This is the best way for my children to become part of the social elite and thereby foster the relationships and influence necessary to effect real and lasting change in this world."*

These are three very distinct Paths, yet all are justifiable in their own way. While perhaps an extreme example, the principle holds true: our North Star doesn't preordain a Path. As it's said, many roads lead to Rome. Our job is to decide which road best suits us.

Paths Can Change

We shouldn't get so marred down in the *how* that we lose sight of the *why*. If one avenue isn't panning out, shift strategies. As Mark Twain wrote in *A Connecticut Yankee in King Arthur's Court*, "She was wise, subtle, and knew more than one way to skin a cat."[1] For instance, look once again at the example of our young college student. A degree is far from the only way to increase his earning potential. There are many highly skilled trades out there that are in demand and rake in the dough. If this person's *why* is to focus on raising a happy, thriving, successful family, then one career is like another, so long as it meets the person's financial needs. In fact, earning a lot of money in and of itself may not necessarily be a requirement in reaching his *why*. Living a modest, simple, debt-free life could negate the need to sacrifice time with the family and spend 60 hours a week in a cubicle.

We also don't want to close ourselves off to what I like to call *happy accidents*. Sometimes things don't go according to plan, and that's okay. Sometimes greater value can be found in the failure than had we succeeded. When Columbus set off from Spain he was looking for a new trade route to India. Epic fail! But a funny thing happened on the way to the Indian forum. He found himself in the "new" world! Considering his *why* was to establish new trade routes and add to the wealth of his backers (not to mention his own coffers), I'm willing to bet ol' Chris didn't sit around wallowing in the depths of depression, having failed in his *how*. He was probably too busy reveling in his *why*.

You Can Have More Than One Path

Years ago friend of mine had just turned 14 when she was in a tragic auto accident. She was asleep in the back seat when another driver careened into her father's car. The accident left her paralyzed from the neck down. In the hospital the prognosis was grim. The doctors said there was little if any hope that she'd ever have any sort of mobility ever again. I would say, "You can imagine how she felt," but I really wonder if we can.

Now like any other 14-year-old girl, my friend had life ambitions—ambitions that didn't include losing mobility. She had a goal—a Path—to earn a university degree and build a successful business career. The accident didn't change any of that; it just added an additional Path: to get healthy. She didn't eliminate her other goals; she added to them, which may seem counterintuitive to the message of this book, but bear with me.

For the next four years nothing mattered but regaining some level of mobility, so she put her education on a life support and dedicated herself to her physical therapy. We're talking four years of intense physical effort, six days a week, ten hours a day. She still graduated from high school with her class—barely, and with a lot of help for her tutors—but graduate she did. It wasn't that education didn't matter, it just didn't matter as much as her health. The good news is the effort paid off, and eventually she regained some limited mobility. She was confined to a wheelchair, but a wheelchair has wheels, and wheels meant freedom! So she cut back on her physical therapy and this time turned her energies toward her education.

Over the next eight years she earned a bachelor's degree from a prestigious university. Granted, eight years was a long time, but this didn't deter her. After earning her undergrad she went on to earn her Master's, spending another two years on this important Path. During that time she still directed some of her energies toward her therapy (hence the eight-year four-year degree), but not nearly as much. Once again, it wasn't that therapy didn't matter, it just didn't matter as much as earning her degrees. She didn't want to let the accident and her condition define her life. She wanted to excel in other things besides only physical therapy, so she applied herself diligently to her studies. It was all about balance, she would later tell me.

> *"She never gave up on any of her Paths. She simply had to put dials on them and turn them back and crank them up as life dictated."*

After graduating my friend set her sights on her third Path and went off to work as a business analyst for the largest, most successful semiconductor company in the world. There she worked 60-hour weeks and commuted long distances to make this dream come true. Therapy was still a Path, but one which was very much on hold. She hadn't given up hope, but it was time to dedicate herself to her current Path—a thriving career.

Eventually though, as is the case for all of us, the environment changed and she had an opportunity to once again assess her Paths. After a decade with her company, she decided it was time to turn her attention back to her health. She left the corporate world, accepted a position with a university, and made physical therapy a primary driver once again.

Today my friend is seeing great progress, which is tremendous. But what's more, she lives a full life, knowing that she never gave up on any of her Paths. She simply had to put dials on them and turn them back and crank them up as life dictated. Physical health, mobility, a world-class education, and a successful career. She's successful on all fronts because she knew how to manage her Paths.

In Summary

1. **Your Path is your *how*:** If your North Star is your *why*—why you do what you do—then your Path is your *how*—how you're going to make your way to your North Star. Paths give form to your North Star, telling you how you're going to accomplish your purpose.

2. **Paths can change:** Life takes you in many different directions. You need to be flexible and willing to allow life's circumstances to move you closer to your purpose in its own way.

3. **You can have more than one Path:** Life isn't about focusing on one activity; it's about adjusting the dials.

Your Turn

Now that you know what North Star guides your actions and decisions, it's time to figure out how you're going to approach your *why*. This means answering questions such as these. (HINT: If these questions sound a lot like the work you did in chapter four when you discovered your guiding principles, strengths, weaknesses, and other personal drivers, you're right. This is no accident. By using what you discovered in chapter four you can begin to develop your Path. So read through what you wrote down and see how it can help guide you.):

▶ What are you going to do to pursue your *why*?

_____

_____

_____

_____

_____

_____

_____

_____

▶ What are the skills and competencies you can bring to this endeavor?

_____

_____

_____

_____

_____

_____

_____

▶ What will be your guiding philosophy?

_____

_____

_____

_____

_____

_____

_____

_____

▶ What's most important to you, and how can you represent this in a Path?

_____

_____

_____

_____

_____

_____

_____

_____

In looking at the answers to these questions, it's a fair bet that what you've found is your Path is determined by what you just plain like to do—those activities that motivate and excite you. Use this as a starting point and you'll be set.

3. Your Destination – Your Long-Term Objective

Where do you see yourself in two or three years? The question is cliché in job interviews, meetings with school counselors, strategic planning sessions in cramped off-site meeting rooms, and stern conversations between parents and floundering children. Nevertheless, the question is key to performing with intent. It's the *intent* part of the equation. Without an understanding of where we want to go, the intent is muddled and confused.

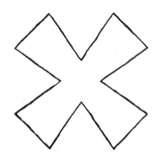

If Lewis and Clark's *why* was to blaze a trail for future expansion of the country, and their *how* was to travel west by land and water, then their Destination was the northwest Pacific Ocean. Our young college student, driven by a *why* of raising a happy, thriving, successful family, selecting a *how* of increasing his earning potential, could have a Destination of a earning a college degree.

A Destination is a *long-term objective*—a goal we set out before ourselves, often times looking out several years. It's the objective we know is necessary for us to move along our Path. What if Lewis and Clark hadn't had a clear Destination? It's a big country. It's not like the northwest was the only place they could have ended up. West to what would eventually become California could certainly have been an option. Southwest could have taken them down through the heart of Spanish territory. There were countless possibilities, so it was important the two explores had a good idea where they were heading—they needed to know where their 'X' marked the spot. The need for a clear Destination is no less urgent for our student. We already pointed out that there are any number of ways he could increase his earning potential without a college degree, but even once committing to university, the question of a major is important to set forth as a Destination. Many smart, well-meaning students have spent five or six years working on their four-year degrees, all because the Destination wasn't clear (yours truly included). Only with a clear definable and measurable Destination in place can we set our sights on the goal.

While a North Star and Path can feel a little nebulous, described in broad sweeping terms, a Destination tends to be much more specific. As we'll see, it can be expressed in almost physical terms with a clear understanding of what success looks like. Indeed, it's this part of the *Planning* phase that gets particularly exciting!

The S.M.A.R.T. Way to Write Objectives

In project and people management circles there's a favorite acronym that can help us better understand what goes into a long-term objective: S.M.A.R.T.:[1]

Specific	What exactly do we want to accomplish?
Measurable	How will we know we've succeeded?
Attainable	Is our goal reachable, given our available resources?
Relevant	Does it directly support our North Star and Path?
Time-Bound	When are we going to reach this Destination?

With this structure in mind, our college student might have a Destination that goes something like this:

Earn a Bachelor's degree in accounting in the spring, four years from now.

Knowing what we now know, we can see that the objective is S.M.A.R.T.:

▶ **Specific:** Earn a degree in accounting.

▶ **Measurable:** The degree awarded.

▶ **Attainable:** Four years is sufficient time.

▶ **Relevant:** It lines up nicely with his Path and North Star.

▶ **Time-Bound:** Spring, four years from now.

It might look simple enough, but don't be fooled; it's harder than it looks. For example, when I ask my college students what their long-term objectives are they might say something like, "Get a better job." Well it doesn't take more than 90 seconds of interrogation to see that this isn't a S.M.A.R.T. long-term objective. What specifically is a "better job?" How do you measure "better?" What skills and experience will you need for this job? See what I mean? Not a real objective; at best it's a "golly gee, someday" wish. The same can be said of other alleged long-term objectives I often see: "Raise my kids," "Change careers," "Retire in comfort," and so on. These are all admirable goals to be sure, but they're not S.M.A.R.T. objectives.

How "Long-Term" Is a Long-Term Objective?

Traditionally, a long-term objective has a timeline of about three to five years, but timeline is not as important as relevance. The most important thing is for our Destination to reflect our North Star and Path.[2] For example, let's say our North Star is to live a financially-secure life. There are a few ways we can do this—different Paths we can take. One way might be to increase our earning potential. In this case we might set our sights on earning a master's degree, something that generally takes two to three years. On the other hand, an alternative Path could be to live a minimalist lifestyle and to reduce our expenses to the bare minimum. In this case our Destination could be to completely pay off all our debt. This could take many years, maybe even decades. Both Destinations—a two-year master's or a debt-free life after ten years—aligns with the stated North Star and Path, so the time required isn't that important.

How Many Destinations Can You Have?

I'm glad you asked. Very few. Even one distinct Destination per path can be problematic. It's far better if one Destination accommodates multiple paths. Why? Because if we're not careful we're going to start a bunch of plates spinning once again and we'll end up right where we started. The more focused we are on one or two Destinations at a time, the more successful we'll become. Later, when we start getting more and more into the details, it'll become clear that too many Destinations will dilute our finite resources and reduce our effectiveness. So let's be careful not to recreate the prison from which we're fighting to escape.

In the interest of full disclosure, this is something I still struggle with. For many years I've had multiple Destinations: publish my PhD dissertation, complete another Ironman, write a book, and restore my MG Midget. Problem is, this is far too many. I've found that, in addition to my regular job, I can be successful in only one main Destination. I came about this insight the hard way; by failing. My PhD dissertation took me longer than it should have because I was spreading myself too thin. The year I finally did complete it I had my first ever DNF (Did Not Finish) in the Ironman. That same year I made it nowhere in my book or MG. The next year I did another Ironman, this one successfully, but the book and MG still floundered. This year the book is well underway, but my fitness has dropped. I've been a no-show to all of the events I registered for, and the MG is still sitting in the garage untouched. The point is, the more we invest in one or two Destinations the more likely we are to succeed.

In Summary

1. **The Destination is where you want to arrive in the long-term:** Without an understanding of where you want to end up, there's no way you can get where you're trying to go.

2. **S.M.A.R.T.:** Your Destinations should be Specific, Measurable, Attainable, Relevant, and Time-Bound.

3. **Time isn't as important as purposeful intent:** Don't worry about how far out your Destination may be—two years or two decades. The most important thing is for your Destination to reflect your Path and North Star.

4. **Set no more than one or two Destinations:** Too many Destinations will turn into more and more spinning plates. Be careful you don't recreate the prison from which you're fighting to escape.

Your Turn

Is it starting to feel real now? It should. Now it's time for you to decide where you're going in the long-term as you start down the Path to your North Star. As you do this, consider the following questions:

▶ What do you need to accomplish to make your way down your Path? Do you need an education? Do you need to lose weight and get fit? Do you need to get out of debt? Do you need to plan for retirement? What Destination—long-term objective—is going to move you closer to your North Star?

_____

_____

_____

_____

_____

_____

_____

▶ What course of action would reflect your highest self—reflect the highest potential you could achieve?

_____

_____

_____

_____

_____

_____

_____

▶   What have you always wanted to do or accomplish but were too unsure of
    yourself to try?

_____

_____

_____

_____

_____

_____

_____

_____

It's time to set your sights down your Path and imagine the success waiting
for you on the other side. It's there, I promise. All you need to do is have the
courage to go after it.

4. Your Milestones – Your Short-Term Objectives

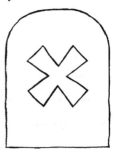

Back in the early days of Europe the Romans laid roads all throughout the empire to move soldiers and supplies quickly and efficiently to wherever they were needed. To help plan the transport of these resources, the Romans marked every thousandth double-step with a large cylindrical stone. The Latin for thousand is *mille*. As it turns out, a thousand double-steps came out to about 1618 yards. Later the British would change this to 1760 yards to equal one *mile*. All this resulted in the term with which we are familiar today: Milestone.[1]

The journey to any great achievement is marked by a series of smaller accomplishments that tell us we're on the right track. These are often called *short-term objectives*—goals we need to reach to work our way toward our long-term objectives. Driving cross-country, we might mark our progress by certain cities or landmarks. An Ironman triathlete may set time goals for each of the three events, the two transitions, and cut-off times. Of course Milestones aren't always physical distance indicators. Our minimalist working on erasing all his debt can set each credit card as a Milestone. Starting with the highest-interest cards first, or perhaps those with the smallest balance, he can pay each one off; each one a Milestone to a debt-free life. It doesn't matter what Milestones we set up, so long as they track progress toward the Destination. For example:

▶ A writer with a Destination of completing a novel in a year can have a Milestone of writing 5,000 words a week.

▶ A swimmer with a Destination of making the Olympic team in two years can have a Milestone of cutting two seconds from her time by the end of the season.

▶ A person with a Destination of losing 100 pounds in one year can have a Milestone of losing four pounds a month.

What we set as our Milestones is not nearly as important as how well they move us in the right direction and motivate us to keep putting in the effort. There are several ways Milestone can do this, so let's explore them a bit.

Chances to Celebrate

Milestones are a great way not only to chart our progress but to celebrate what we've done as well. This helps us reaffirm that we're equal to the challenge. As the adage goes, what gets measured gets done; what gets rewarded gets done. Milestones are a brilliant way for us to do both. They allow us to measure our progress and reward ourselves for the accomplishment. What do I mean by celebrate? We'll talk more about that later, but a reward doesn't have to be expensive or grandiose to be effective. In fact they can be remarkably small, and still pack a wallop. Something as simple as allowing ourselves to indulge in a favorite activity guilt-free can go a long way.

Build Credibility with Your Supporters

Hitting our Milestones also helps us build credibility with our supporters. As they see us hitting our marks, they'll feel more inclined to entrust us with their own limited resources.[2] In this way success breeds success. The more people see us excel, the more they'll want to help us grow even further. Our success becomes their success, and this motivates them to remain and even increase their support and engagement.[3]

S.M.A.R.T. Applies Here As Well

Just as our Destination—our long-term objective—should be Specific, Measurable, Attainable, Relevant, and Time-Bound, so must our Milestones. The only difference (really more of a nuance) is while Destinations are relevant to the Path, Milestones are relevant to the Destination. For instance, our young accounting major has a Destination of earning a bachelor's degree in the spring, four years from now. A Milestone moving him closer to this objective may be to take a full load of 15 credit hours this fall and earn a 3.9 GPA. This meets all the requirements of a S.M.A.R.T. objective.

How "Short-Term" Is a Short-Term Objective?

Odds are you already know the answer to this. Just as in the duration of a long-term objective isn't as important its relevance to the North Star and Path, the right length of time for a Milestone all depends on where we're going. A college degree has built-in Milestones in the form of terms and semesters. On the other hand, America's journey to the moon took considerably longer than four years divided into semesters. From 1961, when President Kennedy first set forth the challenge of landing a man on the moon and returning him safely to Earth, to 1969, when Neil Armstrong first set foot on the moon's surface, many smaller accomplishments—Milestones—marked the journey to this final Destination. For instance, to name a few:

▶ **February 20, 1962:** John Glenn orbited Earth three times.

▶ **October 3, 1962:** Walter Schirra orbited Earth six times.

▶ **July 31, 1964:** Ranger 7 transmitted the first close-up images of the moon back to Earth.

▶ **June 3, 1965:** Edward White performed America's first spacewalk.

▶ **June 2, 1966:** Surveyor 1 soft-landed on the moon.

▶ **December 21, 1968:** Astronauts Frank Borman, James Lovell, and Williams Anders aboard Apollo 8 orbited the moon ten time then returned safely to Earth—gool ol' terra ferma.[4]

Each one of these events was a marvelous technological feat in its own right and was rightfully celebrated, but in the end they were mere Milestones to the ultimate Destination.

How Many Milestones Can You Have?

When it comes to Milestones we need not be quite so draconian. The more into the detail we get, the more broadly we can cast our net—but not too broadly. Remember the plates.

So what might this look like? Let's return to our college student. One of his Milestones may be to take a full load of 15 credit hours this fall and earn a 3.9 GPA. But in addition to this he may set a Milestone to submit all of his assignments on time. He can also commit to reading all of his instructor's feedback and finding ways to improve his performance. All three of these Milestones would help him move closer to his Destination.

In Summary

1. **The Milestones is where you want to arrive in the short-term:** Milestones set the short-term objectives that mark your progress toward your Destinations—your long-term objectives.

2. **Take the time to celebrate:** What gets measured gets done; what gets rewarded gets done. This is the magic of Milestones.

3. **S.M.A.R.T.:** Milestones are really nothing more than shorter Destinations, so make sure they're Specific, Measurable, Attainable, Relevant, and Time-Bound—perhaps even more so.

4. **Time isn't as important as relevance:** The most important thing is that your Milestones should track your progress toward your Destination.

5. **You can have more than one Milestone:** But be careful you don't overload yourself. Remember your limitations.

Your Turn

That's right, it's time to get this on paper. Look at your Destinations and figure out what Milestones you need to reach to accomplish your goals.

► What do you need to do to reach your Destination? What small short-term accomplishments will help you reach greater success?

_____

_____

_____

_____

_____

_____

_____

► Is there a specific sequence you need to follow? For example, if your Destination is to transition careers then there may be certain degrees or certifications you need. This means there may be some courses you need to take to earn these certifications.

_____

_____

_____

_____

_____

_____

_____

▶ What low-hanging fruit can you target to jumpstart the process? For instance, if you're working on getting out of debt, there may be some low-balance credit cards you can wipe out in fairly short order.

_____

_____

_____

_____

_____

_____

_____

_____

▶ What obstacles do you see waiting in the wings? What can you do to address these before they become serious barriers?

_____

_____

_____

_____

_____

_____

_____

_____

Piece by piece you're going to reach your Destination, all because you took the time to figure out what Milestones you needed to set up for your journey.

5. Your Steps – Your Progress Indicators

There's a joke among marathoners.

> *"How in the world can you run 26 miles?"*
>
> *"I don't know. Can you run one mile?"*
>
> *"Sure."*
>
> *"Good. Do that 26 times and you'll run a marathon."*

Okay, a marathon is 26.2 miles, but that doesn't sound as poetic.

Even the most epic journeys can be measured in small, seemingly mundane increments. As Lao Tzu once said, "Do the difficult things while they are easy and do the great things while they are small. The journey of a thousand miles begins with one step."

Up until now everything has been focused on planning. Our North Star gives us purposeful direction. Paths give form to our North Star, telling us how we're going to accomplish our purpose. Our Destinations give us long-term objectives, and our Milestones give us short-term objectives. All this is important and has given us purposeful intent. But now it's time to act; now it's time to take the Steps we need to perform.

Steps Are Where the Rubber Meets the Road

A good Step is something that can be observed and delivers an outcome. College students complete assignments, athletes train, writers write, and employees perform tasks. These are all observable actions, each delivering some kind of result. The size of these results isn't important, only the purposeful intent. In time even tiny results will build, and before we know it we're on our way to accomplishing our Milestones and Destinations. But to get there we have to take that first small Step.

What makes this a particularly powerful concept is that it can give tremendous weight to seemingly insignificant tasks. There's a story (most likely apocryphal, but as Mark Twain is said to have remarked, "Never let the truth stand in the way of a good story") in which President Kennedy was visiting NASA headquarters. While touring the facility he saw a janitor mopping the floor. The president introduced himself and asked the man what he was doing (as though it wasn't obvious). With a straight face the janitor replied, "I'm helping to put a man on the moon!" Okay, so the story's hokey, but don't discount the lesson it has to teach us. Mopping the floor may be tedious if we look at it in isolation, but put it in context of the larger Destination—the moon—and all of a sudden it takes on a more noble quality.

Tangible Progress You Can See

Like Milestones, Steps give evidence to our progress and motivate us to keep going. Seeing tangible daily progress feeds our sense of achievement, which in turn motivates us to keep striving forward. Studies conducted by Harvard researcher Teresa Amabile suggest that seeing daily progress is one of the most important motivators in our performance. It may feel counterintuitive, but seemingly mundane workday events can make or break our momentum as we move toward reaching our Milestones.[1] What's more, the closer we get to achieving a Milestone, the harder we're willing to work to get there. For example, Columbia University's Ran Kivetz conducted a study using coffee-shop rewards cards. The researchers found that as cardholders got closer to that tenth punch (needed to get that free cup of joe), folks increased the frequency of their purchases, all to get that final reward. This psychological mechanism is called *goal gradient* and helps explain why setting small daily Steps can create such momentum.[2] I often experience this goal gradient effect when editing a book. At first the thought of trudging through 300 pages riddled with errors for the fourth time feels like some weird kind of self-flagellation. It needs to be done though, so I set a simple Step of editing five pages a day. In the beginning that's all I can manage. Mustering the intestinal fortitude to do anything more is difficult. But after I reach the halfway point I can see the light at the end of the tunnel, and I become motivated. Now it's nothing to do ten or more pages a day. It becomes all consuming. The closer to the end I get, the more motivated I am to get there.

Steps Can't Be Too Small, but They Can Be Too Large

Okay, *can't* is a strong word, but stay with me. A small Step is still moving us closer to our Milestone, albeit slowly, whereas an overwhelmingly large Step often goes missed or even ignored. Let's say we're working on getting physically fit. A small Step may be to exercise ten minutes each day, maybe walk around the block. That may sound too small to be of any consequence, but ten minutes is better than no minutes. Besides, ten minutes is very likely to be done. On the other hand, if we set a goal of exercising for two hours, odds are much higher that we'll procrastinate the task away and never get around to it. Sure, two hours would have been better than ten minutes, but ten minutes accomplished will always beat two hours never done. Amabile's research found that the most damaging threat to us achieving our goals is experiencing setbacks.[3] If we insist over and over on setting large Steps we'll run the risk of becoming demoralized. Momentum is a key factor in reaching our goals.

S.M.A.R.T. on Steroids

Steps should be S.M.A.R.T. as well—to the extreme. Steps are very unforgiving when we aren't Specific, Measurable, Attainable, Relevant, or Time-Bound. A Step produces a very immediate, observable, and tangible outcome, so there's very little wiggle room. We either completed the Step (completed the assignment, hit the gym, wrote the words, stayed on our diet, etc.) or we didn't. It's very binary. Once again, just as in Destinations are relevant to the Path and Milestones to the Destination, Steps a relevant to the Milestone.

How Many Steps Can You Have?

Ah yes. At this point we can start adding things on. Since a Step only takes a short while to accomplish, we should be able to knock out quite a few over a given period of time. For example, the college student working away on his 15-credit-hour schedule may set several Steps for a single day:

▶ Begin reading chapter three.

▶ Read through the professor's feedback from last week's paper to find opportunities for improvement.

▶ Write an outline for next week's assignment.

▶ Come up with five practice test questions for tomorrow's study group.

When it comes to Steps, the constraint is time, energy, and cognitive resources— all the things we discussed in chapter three. That said, we want to use these finite resources to their full potential. Intelligently-crafted Steps, aligned with our Milestones, will help us do this.

In Summary

1. **Steps are where planning turns to action:** This is where you perform with purposeful intent, put in the hours and take those small Steps that will eventually get you to the top of the mountain.

2. **Steps allow you to see tangible progress:** Seeing tangible daily progress feeds your sense of achievement, which in turn motivates you to keep striving forward.

3. **Success breeds success:** The closer you come to reaching your Milestone, the more motivated you will become to accomplish your Steps.

4. **Small steps completed are better than large steps fumbled:** Setbacks can slow your momentum and cause you to lose motivation. By setting small Steps you increase your odds of success.

5. **S.M.A.R.T.—Very S.M.A.R.T.:** Steps are very unforgiving when you aren't Specific, Measurable, Attainable, Relevant, or Time-Bound.

6. **You can have many Steps:** When it comes to Steps, the constraint is time, energy, and cognitive resources. Fit in all that make sense, given your available resources.

Your Turn

This is when it all gets real. Up until now we've been talking about planning, but now we're also talking about doing. Sure, you'll need to plan out your Steps, but now it's with the specific intent of seeing them done—and in short order. No more hiding or pretending. Now's the time to put up or shut up. So with that, mull over these questions in your notebook:

▶ As you look at your Milestones, what can you do this week—even today— to help move the ball down the field?

_____

_____

_____

_____

_____

_____

_____

▶ When you accomplish something you set out to do that day, how does it make you feel? Write down how it feels to accomplish something you wanted to get done so you can remind yourself of the feeling that awaits each and every day.

_____

_____

_____

_____

_____

_____

▶ Do you find yourself setting daily or weekly goals that are too big and so don't get done? How can you pare these back so they become easier to do?

_____

_____

_____

_____

_____

_____

_____

_____

The exciting thing is you're now on your way. If you've mapped everything back to your North Star then your Steps will set you on the right course—today!

PUTTING IT ALL TOGETHER

Meet Amy. Married, two kids, and a rewarding professional career; she's done all right for herself. But like some of us, she often feels like she serves too many masters. Her obligations as a wife and mother weigh heavy on her, as do her work responsibilities. She wants to be there for everyone when they need her, but the demand always seems to exceed supply. She knows this isn't sustainable so she needs to prioritize.

> **In order to properly understand the big picture, everyone should fear becoming mentally clouded and obsessed with one small section of truth.**
>
> – *Xunzi*

Some other things about Amy; she absolutely loves the outdoors. High in the mountains or lost in the desert, sailing on the seas or gliding on the wind, it's all marvelous and wonderful to her. It feeds her sense of reverence for the planet and piques her curiosity at every turn. She has always felt that the best classroom is outside, not inside. She's also extremely responsible when it comes to finances. Like the rest of us, she and her husband have all kinds of financial commitments, but for her, the most important thing she can invest in is her family. This commitment to her family permeates everything she does. Despite her professional success, when asked, she would say the most important thing is to be there for her family and provide them with life-enhancing experiences.

Given the care she holds for her family and her financial conservatism, it may come as no surprise that she has a relatively low tolerance for risk. One would never call her squeamish; she's an adventurous type that doesn't let grass grow under her feet. But she's not going to become tomorrow's next adrenaline junky. Taking chances feels like an unnecessary risk to herself and her family. One can explore the world without incurring broken bones. Simply put, Amy's the kind of person who takes life by the horns, but makes sure the horns are corked.

These are Amy's guiding principles—the values that direct her decisions. With this in mind, let's look at how Amy maps out her North Star, Path, Destination, Milestones, and Steps:

North Star:

The North Star tells us what's most important to us and why. It sets the tone for the lives we want to live. In the case of our friend Amy, her guiding principles point her toward this North Star:

> *Live a life of curiosity, reverence, appreciation, and respect for the environment, all while providing my family with opportunities to responsibly and safely experience all that life holds.*

See how this North Star supports her guiding principles? Love of the outdoors, its ability to enrich one's life, devotion to her family, and a nod toward sensibility? All her guiding principles are clearly represented in her North Star.

Path:

If our North Star is our *why*—why we do what we do—then our Path is our *how*—how we're going to track our journey toward our North Star. Paths give form to our North Star, telling us how we're going to accomplish our purpose. For Amy, she has the following Path:

> *Take the family on regular outdoor excursions that provide meaningful life experiences—experiences that instill a love and reverence for the environment and one another.*

This Path draws a clear and intentional trajectory toward Amy's North Star. By following this Path she'll be living a life true to herself and her nature. Of course Amy likely has other paths as well, but we'll focus on this one for this example.

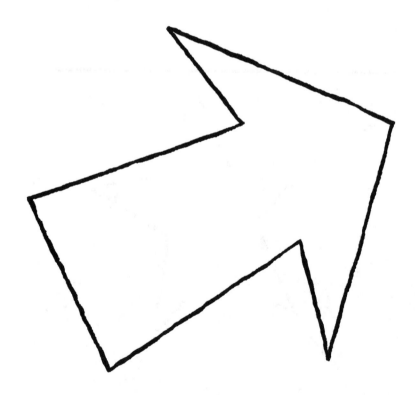

Destination:

Without an understanding of where we want to go, there's no way for us to perform with intent. Our Destination is a long-term objective that moves us along our Path's journey. For Amy, one of her Destinations is as follows:

Take the family on a scuba diving trip in three years.

Once again, the Destination lines up nicely with her Path and North Star. In addition, charting out a three-year plan makes sense for Amy. She's financially responsible and has low tolerance for risk. She'll want to make sure she has all her ducks in a row before committing her family to the deep blue sea.

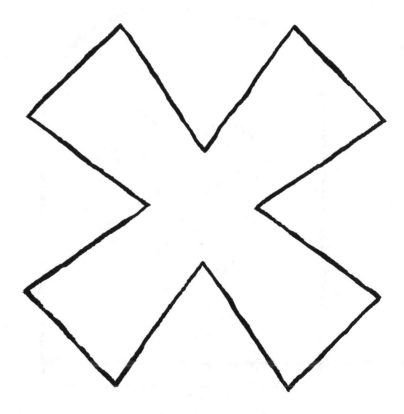

Milestones:

Milestones set the short-term goals that mark our progress toward our Destinations. For Amy's Destination, she has two Milestones, each reflecting different aspects of her North Star and guiding principles:

1. *Get the family safely certified in scuba diving.*

2. *Save enough money so we can go on the trip without going into debt.*

It's no accident that Amy would explicitly state that she wants her family "safely certified." Remember, she's not the sort that would light her hair on fire and jump out of an airplane trailing behind a Red Bull banner. Nor is she the kind that would make foolish financial decisions. As before, we see that Amy is adventurous but deliberate.

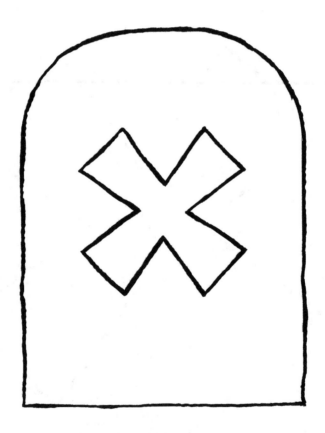

Steps:

This is where we perform with purposeful intent, put in the hours, and take those small Steps that will eventually get us to the top of the mountain (or in the case of Amy, to the bottom of the sea). Remember, flash is not the name of the game here. This is where the real work happens. It may not be fancy or even exciting, but when we put it all together it will get us where we want to go.

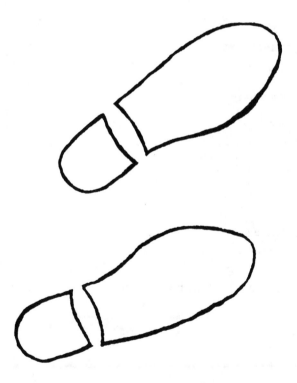

In the case of Amy, she has two Milestones to track to: certifications and funding:

1. **Scuba certification Steps:**

    1. *Identify nearby training schools.*

    2. *Price the available options.*

    3. *Register for classes.*

    4. *Purchase the required gear.*

    5. *Decide if it's better to purchase additional gear or rent it on-site.*

    6. *Arrange family schedules to allow everyone time to take classes.*

    7. *Attend the required classes.*

    8. *Complete the required assignments.*

    9. *Schedule the required open water dives.*

    10. *Pass off all of the final certification tests and requirements.*

2. **Required funds Steps:**

    1. *Set a budget.*

    2. *Decide on a location.*

    3. *Itemize costs.*

    4. *Decide how long the family would like to stay, given the costs.*

    5. *Sit down with the family and establish a savings plan.*

    6. *Begin socking away money every two weeks.*

By performing these small manageable Steps it won't be long before Amy and her family are swimming with the sea turtles and marveling at the abundance of life making its home in the coral reef. (Oh, and getting seasick and puking up their guts over the side of the boat, but that's part of the adventure, kids!)

Bringing It All Together

See the cascading effect? We've moved Amy from big picture, pie-in-the-sky dreaming to specific and clear actions she can take right now to make it all happen. Complete the daily Steps and she'll reach her Milestones. Do this and she'll reach her Destination. All this, in support of her Path and North Star—those things that matter most to her and give her purpose and meaning in life. Looking at it this way it looks easy, doesn't it? Well good news: it is easy. Well, sort of. There are all sorts of things waiting in the wings, dying to get in our way, but more about that later. Right now let's stick with the easy aspect and talk about ways we can make this cascade work for us. To do that, let's talk about how we can make this process work each day.

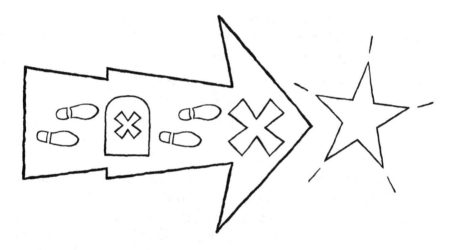

To-Do Lists and Journaling

You've probably noticed a to-do list vibe around this process. This is intentional, but as you can see, it's more than a back-of-the-envelope daily agenda sort of exercise. Think of it in terms of operational planning. Take for instance a ship's log as it navigates the trade routes. A ship's log serves several important purposes. Captains use them to track notable events occurring in and around a ship as it works its way to its destination. These logs track everything concerning the ship's management and operation. They assign and record routine tasks, detail significant events, and evaluate performance on a daily basis. Critically, ship's logs also keep an inventory of the ship's stores and the allocation of its precious resources.[1]

Daily to-do lists and journals serve a similar function for us. They help us track the allocation of our resources and measure the results. Using this approach has many benefits:

▶ **Keeps us focused on what matters:** Each day we must decide how best to allocate our finite resources for the greatest effect. By reviewing what matters most each day we're able to make sure our actions and decisions move us further along our chosen journey.

▶ **Helps us manage our resources:** Making a task list is a great way to remind ourselves that there are only so many hours in the day.

▶ **Helps us reach our objectives:** Research has shown that journaling enables us to better track and reach our objectives by keeping us focused on the goals we've set for ourselves.[2, 3, 4]

▶ **Helps us build on our successes:** When something works well—when we make measurable progress toward a particular goal—we can see what we did to build up to this and apply it to other goals.

▶ **Helps us learn from our failures:** Sometimes things won't go so well. We'll miss our goals or become sidetracked. Our opportunity to learn from these slips is tremendous. We can see where we may have lost focus, misallocated resources, underestimated the task at hand, or any number of lessons we can learn and later apply.

▶ **Helps us kill several birds with one stone:** Looking at all our goals as a whole allows us to look for opportunities to overlap our tasks. For example, writing a book for my consulting firm helps me move the ball forward in terms of developing my consulting business as well as a writing career.

▶ **Reduces stress:** It's easy to become overwhelmed as we think about everything that needs to be done. Parsing out the day's responsibilities in clear, easy-to-execute tasks can help bring method to the madness. In fact, there's even a substantial body of evidence which suggest that keeping a journal can improve our emotional health as we tackle life's challenges and devise solutions.[5]

▶ **Serves as a reminder:** Spinning so many plates can cause us to forget things. By making a list we can stop worrying about remembering and focus on performing.

▶ **Tracks and rewards progress:** Even small, seemingly insignificant rewards can have a positive effect. For each task I accomplish I get a green checkmark, and for each task I miss I get a red X. It may seem small and inconsequential, but filling that box with a big green checkmark is highly rewarding to me. Checking off the day's list can be an effective way of seeing our progress toward the Destination. One of the reasons long-term plans can fail is because we become discouraged. By tracking progress each and every day we see the status bar plugging along, assuring us that we're making small but meaningful steps toward our ultimate goals.

▶ **Fights Procrastination:** Procrastination is often rooted in uncertainty and fear—uncertainty of how to approach a daunting problem and fear that we'll fail in the attempt.[6] Procrastination can also be a learned behavior, a response to a time when we may have been beaten down for taking the initiative.[7] It has also been associated with perfectionism,[8] a topic we'll discuss later. Not only does goal-setting reduce procrastination,[9] but breaking the goal down into small, simple, manageable steps is a great way to boost our confidence, showing us that we can do the work and fight that menace: procrastination.[10]

▶ **Provides a healthy pursuit of self-esteem:** In a study done to evaluate the effects of the pursuit of self-esteem on our ability to thrive in the workplace, close to half the participants reported that accomplishing tasks, no matter how small, helped them feel a sense of confidence and achievement.[11] It's not a hard concept to grasp: when we accomplish things, we feel good.

But Also, Beware of the Traps of To-Do Lists

In his book, *The One Thing*, Gary Keller casts a suspicious eye on most to-do lists,[12] as well he should. Some time back I was between clients, which meant I had a lot of time on my hands (and more than a little stress and anxiety). I had bills to pay just like everyone else, so sitting around and binge-watching Netflix wasn't going to be part of my success strategy. Luckily I had my Destination, Milestones, and Steps to work toward, so I wasn't lost on the seas without a rudder. But with all this time available, I should be at least two or three times as productive as usual, right? So I pulled out my journal and loaded it up. Where normally I might commit to four or five tasks for each day, I scrawled out somewhere between 15 to 20 to-do items. For weeks I was a blur, running this way and that, feeling oh so productive. But after a while I started to feel frenzied and stressed. I found myself feeling resentful of how busy I was, that I never had a free moment to myself, that I was a slave to more task masters than I could count. Then it struck me. Who were these taskmasters? No one who I didn't invite in to harangue me, that's who! And whose fault was it that I had so much to do each day? Once again, my own. And the value of what I was doing? Very, very dubious. As I analyzed my list I realized that most of the to-do items were little better than make-work assignments—things designed to simply help me feel busy. But the most striking revelation came when I looked at what I had actually accomplished, which as it turned out was precious little. All the little, easy, yet ultimately useless things had drowned out what really mattered. In my desire to feel busy and productive during this time of unemployment I had lost sight of my North Star and turned myself into an aimless whirling dervish.

There's a world of difference between a to-do list full of "could do's" and a success list full of "should do's."[13] The list should keep us laser-focused on what's most important, not be a laundry list of things we can do to help us feel busy.

How I Use My Journal

There's no one right way to use a journal as we chart our progress. Even my own methods have evolved over time, and no doubt will continue to change in the future. I know some people who keep such detailed journals that they put my pathetic scribblings to shame, but that doesn't matter. How you use your journal isn't nearly as important as how well and often you use it.

As I map out my journaling process it may help if I explain what kind of tools I use. To start with, I'm sort of old fashioned. I like notebooks—real notebooks with heavy crisp paper and leather binding. I like the feel and smell of it as I going about my daily routines. I also like to use different types of pens. I'm no artist, that's for darn sure, but I like the thought that my journal is a tangible piece of work I'm crafting over time. I know, I know, this all sounds very artsy-fartsy, hoity-toity—very not-me—but that's okay. I like it and that's important. Journaling needs to be an activity you look forward to in and of itself. So with that in mind, use whatever tools work best for you—that speak to you: notebooks, computers, tablets, notecards, stone carvings—it's all up to you.

Okay. With that out of the way, let's talk about how I use my notebook:

Each Year

At the end of each year, around Christmas, I write down my Paths for the following year. Each one of these Paths represents a track I then follow throughout the year. For me personally, I have five tracks in all: Academic, Writing, Consulting, Avocation, and Fitness. I then set a Destination for each Path. Often times I carry these Destinations over from the previous year. After all, long-term objectives may very well take more than a year to accomplish. Next I set my Milestones for each Destination—my short-term objectives for that year. For example, my writing Path track may look something like this:

1. **Path:** *Pursue my writing career.*

   1. **Destination:** *Publish* The Great American Novel.

      ☐ **Milestone:** *Complete an outline for a 400-page novel by the end of February.*

      ☐ **Milestone:** *Complete a rough draft by the end of June.*

      ☐ **Milestone:** *Complete a first draft edit by the end of October.*

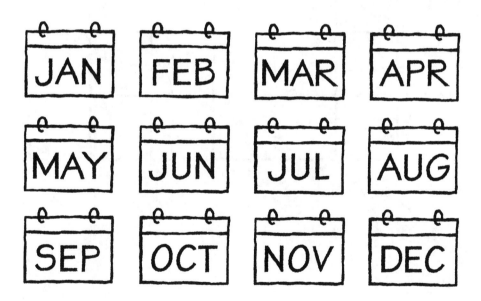

Each Month

At the end of each month I evaluate my progress then decide what I want to accomplish the following month. So if we're at the beginning of January, and I want to develop a complete an outline for a 400-page novel by the end of February, I would set a goal that looks something like this:

☐ **January:** *Create character profiles and draw up a basic outline following the hero's journey story arc.*

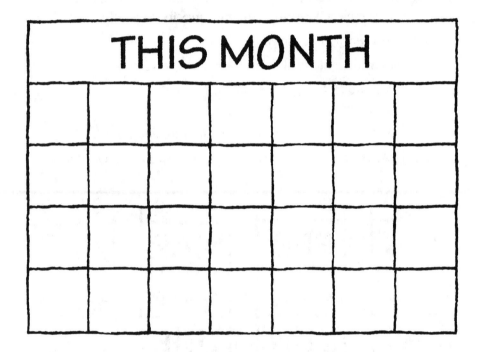

Each Week

At the end of each week I evaluate my progress and determine what I want to accomplish the following week. Following my writing example, I might have something like this:

☐ **This Week:** *Create character profiles for my main protagonist and antagonist.*

S	M	T	W	T	F	S

Each Day

Like the year, month, and week, the day starts the evening before. At the end of each day I plan out what Steps I need to accomplish the following day to make progress toward my Milestones. Depending on the things I want to accomplish that day, I generally list out between three to five Steps. With this in mind, I might do something like this:

- ☐ *Select a name for the protagonist.*
- ☐ *Fill in the general details: gender, age, description, habits, mannerisms, etc.*
- ☐ *Chart out the character's personal development journey, beginning of the story to the end.*

This may be all I list for the day, depending on what else I have going on. If I think I have more time I may include an addition writing Milestone, or I may put one or two Steps from another Path. On the other hand, if the day's pretty maxed-out then this is all I may commit to. Remember, this isn't a to-do list; it's a list of things I want to accomplish that move me closer to my goals.

Throughout the Day

My journal goes everywhere with me. It's never more than a few feet away, keeping me on track. Each day I open it to the day's Steps and set it next to me. As I accomplish each step I get my reward: the coveted green checkmark! The green checkmark says, "Excellent, good job! Now on to the next Step." I love the green checkmark. I love it so much I'll do everything I can to earn that "attaboy." Failing to do so comes with a consequence: the red X. The red X says, "Hmmm...got a little distracted, did we? That's a real shame, because now you're no closer to your goal than you were at the beginning of the day." I hate the red X. I'll do everything I can to avoid the red X.

We talked earlier about how what gets measured and rewarded gets done. The green checkmark and the red X are great examples of the simplicity of this principle. Speaking for myself, these small marks in my notebook are extremely effective rewards and punishments. It's like the A+ on an assignment or a gold star on a piece of homework. There's power in these symbols. Select symbols that speak to you and you'll be surprised how much you'll modify your behavior to earn these simple rewards.

Do Whatever Works for You

As you look through my example you may be asking yourself, "Wait. If you have your Milestones listed for the year and your Steps listed for each day, what do you call the goals you have for each month and week?" I don't know; mini-milestones? Long strides? Granted, I have several permutations of goals between Milestones and Steps, but this helps me break my objectives down into manageable pieces. It doesn't change the nature of the process. As I say, this method works for me, but that doesn't mean it's the only way to roll. Feel free to develop your own processes, modify this one, or apply the ideas to any other process you may already have in place. It's all about doing what best meets your own particular style. It doesn't matter what you do, so long as you do it. A "good-enough" process implemented is better than a "stellar" process never moved from the drawing board.

In Summary

1. **Cascading from big-picture dreams to specific tasks makes it all happen:** The logical sequence of performing small simple tasks directed toward a meaningful purpose enables you to accomplish great things.

2. **To-do lists and journaling keep you focused:** These tools help you train your attention on what matters. They manage your resources, build on your successes, help you learn from your failures, fight procrastination, and increase your self-esteem.

Your Turn

Planning, planning, planning. This is a lot of planning. Depending on your perspective, planning your personal and professional life in such meticulous detail may seem like a no-brainer or a nonstarter. Let's find out which it is for you and see what we can do:

▶ What do you like about planning?

_____

_____

_____

_____

_____

_____

_____

_____

▶ What do you dislike about planning?

_____

_____

_____

_____

_____

_____

_____

► Have you ever planned something out in great detail, such as a trip, a vacation, or a home-improvement project? How did that activity turn out? How did planning help you be successful?

_____

_____

_____

_____

_____

_____

_____

► Have you ever forgone the planning phase and jumped right into something? How did that work out for you? Could a little planning upfront have made the experience better? How so?

_____

_____

_____

_____

_____

_____

_____

The key in all of this is to make friends with your own planning style so it works for you. If you're more of an adventurous type, call it *mapping* or *charting* instead of *planning*. Or if you're an avid traveler, call it your *itinerary*. The point is this: make it your own and so you'll look forward to spending time with it.

CHAPTER 7: TAKE ACTION
(with intent)

Patience and perseverance have a magical effect before
which difficulties disappear and obstacles vanish.

– John Quincy Adams
American statesman, sixth President of the United States

As part of the great move west, members of the Church of Jesus Christ of Latter
Day Saints (the Mormons) began arriving in the Great Salt Lake valley in 1847.
However, the church wanted to establish a strong presence in the region east
of the Colorado River, so it organized the San Juan mission and tasked it with
establishing a settlement down south.

In April of 1879 a scouting party set off to find a suitable site. They found one
at the mouth of Montezuma Creek on the San Juan River. But getting there
wasn't going to be easy. The pioneers had two options: a trip of nearly 500 miles
around what would later be called Glen Canyon, or a short-cut that would take
them through the canyon. After some deliberation they chose the canyon route,
which in addition to being shorter, the scouts figured was simpler as well. So the
expedition, consisting of 250 men, women, and children, 83 wagons, and over
1,000 head of livestock, gathered on November 1879 and began the journey.

As it turned out, the "short-cut" proved to be more than they had bargained
for. They came up against an area that would become known as "Hole-in-the-
Rock," a narrow crack in the canyon rim 2.5 miles downstream from the mouth
of the Escalante River. It was a precipitous drop to the river below, nearly 2,000
feet with an average grade of 25 degrees (some places as steep as 45 degrees).
It was through this narrow steep notch in the canyon wall that the party would
need to thread their way if they were going to continue on their trek.

Throughout the winter the group worked on the crack, enlarging the opening so the wagons and livestock could pass through. Work was slow, tedious, and frustrating. All they had to work with were a few pick axes, shovels, and some blasting powder. But eventually the team was ready, and on January 26, 1880, the expedition made its way slowly down the precarious road.

Miraculously, no lives were lost. After long months of hard work and deprivation, the party eventually reached the San Juan River and built their settlement. Today this area is known as Bluff, Utah. Granted, a journey that should have taken six weeks took six months, but in the end the pioneers won.

Today most of the original Hole-in-the-Rock trail is still visible and is listed on the National Register of Historic Places.[1] Ironically, what was once an impediment became a thoroughfare as the Hole-in-the-Rock road continued to be used as the primary link between Bluff and Salt Lake City for several years. This may sound like a side note, but it's not. I believe the work we put into overcoming obstacles will pay off far into the future, well past the particular challenge of the moment.

All this brings me to an important point, and that is even when we have a purpose, a plan, and bring the right tools to the party, we're going to encounter obstacles. No journey worth taking ever came without hurdles to overcome. And believe me, we're going to encounter plenty. In this chapter we're going to explore some of the roadblocks that may impede our progress. We're also going to figure out ways to move the boulders and get the wagon train moving again.

The last step on the ADEPT Model is all about taking purposeful action and clobbering those things that would try to distract us from our goals. What follows are some things we can do to help us perform with intent:

1. Create Purposeful Habits

2. Schedule a Buffer

3. Keep Your Supporters Cheering

4. Abandon the Myth of Multitasking

5. Strive for Progress; Not Perfection

6. Embrace the Serenity Prayer

7. Learn From Your Failures

8. Beware of Overload, Stress, and Anxiety

9. Keep it All in Perspective

10. Enjoy the Journey

1. CREATE PURPOSEFUL HABITS

It's hard to underestimate the power of habits, either for good or ill. Habits have this way of taking deliberate thought out of the equation and setting our behavior on autopilot. As a result we can do some pretty complex things without nary a brain cell dedicated to the effort. Take driving, for instance. It's so easy

> We are what we repeatedly do. Excellence, then, is not an act, but a habit.
>
> – *Aristotle*

we can do it while eating, listening to music, and talking with our passengers. Yet teach a 15-year-old how to drive and one quickly realizes how much our good driving skills are based on habit. Teaching a young driver requires us to break things down into basic elements—elements we haven't thought about in years—and explain them in excruciating detail.

Creating habits around complex actions comes with valuable dividends. Habits require less cognitive resources, thus freeing our minds up for more aspirational activities. They also make the quality of the outcome more consistent. Habits are, to a tremendous degree, why winners always win. It's habit. Hours of practice, training, envisioning, doing, and thinking of little else; winning for these high performers becomes more of an inevitability than a possibility. On the other hand, habits have a dark side, something I'm sure we're all familiar with. Just as habits can make winning more of an inevitability than a possibility, bad habits make mediocrity something close to a foregone conclusion. The lesson here isn't hard to see: develop good habits and ditch the bad ones.

How to Get Your Habits to Work for Your

In his book, *The Power of Habit: Why We Do What We Do in Life and Business*, Charles Duhigg explores a very simple yet powerful cycle that drives our habits. He demonstrates how a *cue* initiates a *routine* which is then supported by a *reward*. This creates a habit.[1] Let's see how this pattern can help us perform with intent:

Recognizing an Unproductive Habit

1. **Routine:** The first step is to identify the routine that's distracting us from performing with intent. For example, let's say we want to get physically fit and eat better—nix the junk food and eat more healthful foods. But we notice something. We realize that after every meal we want a treat, some kind of sweet to top of the meal. It's not a big deal, until we figure out that this practice is adding over 300 calories a day to our diet. Eating a treat after each meal is a routine we need to address.

2. **Cue:** With our routine defined, the next step is to identify the cues that initiate this behavior. This may not be as easy as it sounds. The cue may be rooted in where we are, the time of day, our emotional state, the people around us, or even what happened moments before. To make things even more complicated, in many cases our cue may very well be a combination of these factors. In the case of eating a treat, maybe the cue is conditioning. Like Pavlov's dog, our brains may be conditioned to want something sweet after eating. Maybe it's a reward we give ourselves for eating a healthful meal, a little "attaboy" we've earned for making good food choices. Maybe it's part of a social thing, something that bonds us with friends or family. Identifying the cue is important because it helps us understand the real root of our behavior.

3. **Reward:** Finally, recognize what rewards come about from this behavior. In the case of eating sweets, maybe they make us feel good and sated. Maybe they bring about childhood warm fuzzies. Maybe it's an act of defiance, a sort of "I'm-an-adult-and-I-can-eat-what-I-want" gesture. When we understand the nature of the reward we'll be better able to replace it with something more purposeful.

Once we have a good idea what habits are distracting us from performing with intent, the circumstances that trigger these behaviors, and the rewards we derive from these routines, we can then set about rewiring our habitual lives.

Replacing an Unproductive Habit with a Purposeful Habit

1. **Routine:** Decide what sort of routine we want to establish. For example, let's once again return to the routine of eating a treat after each meal. We want to replace this with a new, more positive routine. So let's try this: after each meal, instead of having a treat, we allow ourselves some other indulgence—something we enjoy but doesn't work against us. In fact, let's find something that works *for* us and our goal of getting fit. What sort of indulgence? That all depends on you, but for the sake of this example let's say we allow ourselves a ten-minute walk, listening to our favorite music— that band that we love but makes those around us groan. (You know, like Rush.) By doing this we remove a routine that's working against our goal of getting fit and replace it with something that works in our favor.

2. **Cue:** Find a cue or a trigger that already exists on which you can stack this new routine. The best kind of trigger is an existing behavior that has staying power. The great thing about using eating as a cue is that we all eat, several times a day in fact, last I checked. Furthermore, this cue is already directly tied to the undesirable behavior. All we need to do is replace one response to the cue with another. Regardless of what you select as a cue, do so deliberately. Decide that whenever this cue occurs you're going to follow-up with the new would-be habit.

3. **Reward:** The problem with rewards is we often think they need to be big, complex, or even expensive to have the desired effect. Not so. Even small self-talk rewards like saying, "Excellent" after completing a task can have a positive effect. For example, as we walk, listening to our music, we should reward ourselves with positive messages. "This feels great" and "I'm nailing this goal" are great things we can tell ourselves as we work on creating a new routine. For me, there's an energy drink I'm particularly fond of but shouldn't overdo. Whenever I sit down to write I allow myself this drink as a treat. It's a small reward, but one that is just enough to get me at my desk when I might rather do something else.

The great thing about this technique is it takes advantage of what's called *if- then* planning. In her book, *Succeed*, Carol Dweck talks about the simple yet profound power of this process.[2] The idea is this: when *X* happens, we should do *Y*. BJ Fogg keys in on this same principle when he talks about accomplishing big things by changing tiny habits.[3] For Fogg, part of the secret lies in setting *if- then* planning around events that are going to occur naturally and easily, such as getting up in the morning, getting dressed, or something equally as routine and mundane. In the case of the health example above we used eating—one of the most basic and mundane daily acts of survival. By making this our X on which we then attach our Y, we make it easy for us to build these tiny habits.

In Summary

1. **Habits are powerful, so get them to work for you:** Good habits make success more of an inevitability than a possibility. On the other hand, bad habits make mediocrity something close to a foregone conclusion.

2. **Habits can be programmed:** A *cue* initiates a *routine* which is then supported by a *reward*. This process allows you to create purposeful habits.

Your Turn

Habits can be your very best friend when it comes to performing with intent, or your worse enemy, so take the time to figure out how they're helping or hindering you. Here are some questions for you to consider:

▶ What habits are preventing you from performing with intent?

_____

_____

_____

_____

_____

_____

_____

_____

▶ What kinds of rewards are reinforcing these undesirable habits?

_____

_____

_____

_____

_____

_____

_____

_____

► What habits would you like to develop to replace these bad habits?

_____

_____

_____

_____

_____

_____

_____

_____

► What habits are helping you today—habits you can further reinforce to become stronger and more prominent?

_____

_____

_____

_____

_____

_____

_____

_____

Developing purposeful habits can make the entire ADEPT Model more or less run itself on autopilot, so make them count!

2. SCHEDULE A BUFFER

When I was a young man my father and I were in Japan, traveling from Tokyo to Nagoya on the famed *Tokaido Shinkansen*, better known in the US as the Japanese bullet train. We were

Better three hours too soon than a minute too late.

– William Shakespeare

booking along at a brisk 190 km per hour, about 118 mph, but every once in a while the train slowed for whatever reason. As we got started again, I noticed the speed ramped up to 220 km per hour, close to 137 mph. I asked my father, if the train could have been doing 220 km per hour all along, why wasn't it going that speed the entire way. He explained that if the train ran at full speed the whole way then it would inevitably arrive late. Things are bound to happen that would slow the train down, as it had in this instance. Had the train been traveling at full speed then there would be no room to make up for lost time. Sure enough, despite our unscheduled stops, the train arrived at the station precisely at the time printed on our tickets.

For a massive national train network, connecting travelers to an even larger international travel system, punctuality and predictability are paramount. There are additional legs downstream that all need to knit together seamlessly. We're no different. People are relying on us to deliver exactly what we agreed to deliver, precisely when we agreed to deliver it. When we're late we create ripples downstream. This in turn creates stress and anxiety for us as well as others. I don't know about you, but I'm all about reducing stress—especially stress I bring upon myself.

Overestimate Time and Resources Required

So often I hear people say they're behind in something or another and are having to play catch-up. This is fine, but it presumes they have the time and energy necessary in reserve to actually catch up. Quite often these folks are late before they even get started. As legendary coach John Wooden is said to have remarked, "If you don't have the time to do it right, when will you have the time to do it over?"

There's a saying that goes, "If you fail to plan, you plan to fail." There's more to this, however. Sometimes we plan, but fail to plan properly. For example, we often underestimate the amount of time or resources it'll take to get a job done. This is called falling prey to *planning fallacy*. It refers to our propensity to underestimate the amount of time it will take to do something, even when we've done it before and have data to draw upon in making our estimation.[1] The way to beat this is to err on the other side and overestimate the need. By overestimating and building a buffer we'll likely be closer to reality than if we were to follow our calculations.

Coming back to lessons learned from my father, he once told me that estimating the cost of remodeling a room was simple: calculate the costs to the last dollar, he told me, then multiply it by three. That'll likely be closer to the final cost than your careful calculation suggested. (Our Chinese wall designer and his one extra brick would have had a fit at this idea, but there you are.)

Is Being On Time Really That Important?

I understand that punctuality isn't as important to some as it may be to others. I've been around the block a few times and I've encountered more than my fair share of the chronically-tardy. This begs the question: is being on time really all that important, or is this simply me giving voice to one of my pet peeves? Well, maybe it's a little of both, but consider the following: punctuality shows other's that:

▶ We're dependable.

▶ We manage our time well.

▶ We exercise discipline.

▶ We respect the time of others.

▶ We're the masters of our schedules (and not the other way around).

On the other hand, when we're late:

▶ We steal time from others—time they could've been using with purposeful intent to reach their own Desinations.

▶ We start the meeting off on a bad note, marring the experience for everyone.

▶ We strain important relationships.

▶ We show a lack of professionalism and discipline.

Ultimately it doesn't take any more careful planning to be on time versus five minutes late, so why plan on the latter over the former? My father is fond of saying that a full gas tank doesn't cost any more than an empty one. You're going to drive the miles, so it's not like you can go without gas. Whether the money is in your wallet or in your talk, it makes no difference, so fill 'er up.

Likewise, if you can plan on being someplace five minutes late, why not plan to be on time? You know you're going to go, so leave with time to spare. In most cases whatever you're doing that's making you late will be there when you get back, so leave it and focus on the next task at hand.

In Summary

1. **Schedule a buffer:** When you're late you create ripples downstream, which in turn creates stress and anxiety for yourself as well as others.

2. **Overestimate time and resources required:** By overestimating the time necessary and building a buffer you'll probably make it in the nick of time.

3. **Punctuality shows respect for others:** Not to mention professionalism, dependability, discipline, and self-control.

Your Turn

Punctuality is important, not only for your own stress and anxiety level but for the relationships you have with your supporters. With this in mind, ask yourself:

▶ Do you feel stress and anxiety when you're running late?

_____

_____

_____

_____

_____

_____

_____

_____

▶ When people are late meeting you, how does it make you feel? How does it affect how you think about them?

_____

_____

_____

_____

_____

_____

_____

▶ What are some of the ways you cut it too close and create unnecessary stress for yourself and others?

_____

_____

_____

_____

_____

_____

_____

_____

▶ What are some things you can do to build in a buffer and better manage your time?

_____

_____

_____

_____

_____

_____

_____

_____

Of course sometimes you're going to be late. Life happens. But this should be the exception, not the rule. By being on time you show others how important they are to you.

3. KEEP YOUR SUPPORTERS CHEERING

Western culture glorifies the "self-made" man, that intrepid entrepreneur who started with nothing more than the shirt on his back and a buck forty in his pocket. The message

> **No one is self-made.**
>
> – *Gary Keller*

is intended to be inspiring, telling all who would listen that the world is their oyster, that no matter their background or economic circumstances, anyone can make it big. All one needs is a great idea and a work ethic second to none.

There's no arguing this can be an inspiring message, and goodness knows there's an entire heroes gallery who answered the call and reached untold heights as a result. However, if we peel back the curtain a bit we realize that no man is an island. Show me a "self-made" man and I'll show you someone who benefitted from a strong educational system, a government who encouraged economic growth, an army of creditors and backers, a social infrastructure that allowed business to flourish, a customer base who bought into the vision, supporters who cheered him along, and so forth. As His Holiness the Fourteenth the Dalai Lama said, "All of these factors are inextricably linked with other people's efforts and cooperation. Others are indispensable."[1]

Get Your Supporters Engaged

Watch about any *Star Trek* episode and you'll hear the captain order the pilot to engage the thrusters, warp drive, or some other equally cool scifi doohickey. As it so happens, engaging a warp drive is a pretty good analogy for engaging our supporters. To engage something is to commit it to a given cause, process, or event. In the case of the USS Enterprise, the ship can tool along the galaxy on impulse power quite nicely, thank you very much. That's really all it needs, if all it's going to do is lollygag and cruise about. But if the crew really wants to get somewhere, and in a hurry, they must engage an additional resource—the warp drive. Plug that cool little piece of hardware into the system and now we're talking business.

Our supporters can likewise be engaged or (as is all too often the case) disengaged. Oh sure, we can still keep plugging along with minimal input from these folks, but this is really just "keep the lights on" sort of performance. Tap into their passion, their energy, their ambition, and their desire to do something great and we've got warp drive. It's not about tricking or paying them to commit more; it's about giving them something worthwhile to commit to. Remember that support from others is by no means a given. Everyone around us is busy allocating their own finite resources to their own passions and priorities. If we can't tie our own priorities to those of our supporters then their interest will slowly dwindle.

Here are a few things that will help us win and keep supporter engagement:

▶ **Inspire a shared vision for the future:** There are three elements to this first point worth exploring: *Inspire*, *Shared*, and *Vision*.

   Inspire: Simply communicating or delivering a shared vision is not the same as *inspiring* a shared vision. Inspiration wells within us a passion to do marvelous things for little extrinsic reward.

   Shared: When a vision is *shared* it's owned by the community, the cadre, the fraternity, the cabal. It creates a connection that can be powerful indeed.

   Vision: We humans are visionary creatures. We seem to be hardwired to look out into the future and see a path to a better tomorrow.

   All combined, it's not hard to see the power of *inspiring a shared vision of the future*.

▶ **Relate what matters to us to what matters to them:** Just because something matters to us doesn't mean it matters to those whose support we need. To win their help we need to tie what we're trying to do to something that matters to them. This creates a mutually-beneficial symbiotic relationship. By helping us, our supporters help themselves, even if the objectives are not themselves identical.

▶ **Express the value of that future end-state in emotional terms:** Ask any advertiser or marketer and they'll tell you that every decision, every purchase, every action taken is emotionally inspired. In our case, passion and purpose are clearly emotionally-fueled concepts. If we're going to win the support of others we need to first win their hearts. This is done by expressing the end-state in terms that resonate with them emotionally.

▶ **Create a sense of urgency:** As the old adage goes, why put off to tomorrow what you can do today? Thing is, procrastination often reigns supreme, and it's no wonder. We have things all around us screaming for our limited time, energy, and cognitive resources. With these demands in our face right now, it's hard to dedicate time to things that are far in the future. This is why we need to create a sense of urgency. To rally the troops there needs to be a consensus that action is needed—and needed now.

▶ **Involve them throughout the journey:** Supporters are partners in our journey. They're our cheerleaders, champions, sometimes even our therapists. These are people we want every step of the way, not only when we think their contributions are helpful or convenient. Remember, in relating what matters to us to what matters to them we made them serious partners in all that we do. Treat them as such.

▶ **Acknowledge and reward their contributions at each success:** No one likes to be taken for granted, especially those who have given us their emotional and material support. Many of these people have paid dearly for us to succeed, some may have even postponed their own ambitions to help us reach our goals. These are not people we want to treat lightly. Our success is their success as well, and they need to feel that level of appreciation.[2, 3]

Asking Supporters to Embrace Change

In addition to asking for their resources, often times we're asking our supporters to embrace change. For example, if we're perusing a career change, this affects our families in significant ways. They too will need to embrace our new career trajectory. When it comes to those close to us—family, friends, employers, partners, etc.—there's a world of difference between *accepting* change and *embracing* change:

▶ **Accepting Change:** At best, accepting change is passive; at worse it's counterproductive. For example, I accept that when winter hits Utah it's going to be cold and snowy. Thing is, I don't like cold and snowy, so I don't get out and bike or run as much as I'd like. Sure, I have a trainer and treadmill in the basement, but that's not especially exciting. As a result I lose fitness, get fat, and start feeling depressed. I'm not rejecting the change, but I'm not embracing it. Consequently my performance suffers.

▶ **Embracing Change:** By contrast, embracing change means squeezing every ounce of benefit from it we can. For example, those who embrace the change of seasons in Utah celebrate by hitting the slopes with gusto in the winter then jumping on their bikes in the summer. For these folks, each seasonal change brings exciting opportunities that they can hardly wait to exploit. Unlike me, they're rocking their fitness year-round and loving every minute. (How I hate them so.)

If we want to keep our cheerleaders firmly behind us we need to understand and adjust for how our requests for support will affect them. Here are some things we should do to keep our supporters engaged:

▶ **Communicate the Value of Reaching the Goal Through Their Eyes:** We need to help our supporters see the benefits that will come with the change—benefits that matter to those affected by the change personally. It's not enough to simply say our supporters love us and believe in what we're trying to do. Ultimately there needs to be some benefit to them, even if that benefit is to see us happy. For example, my wife and I were paying and sacrificing a great deal for our daughter to attend dance classes. It's something she wanted desperately and begged us to do. Yet every evening when we picked her up she would whine and complain. The teacher did this, the girls did that, her legs hurt, her feet hurt, etc. On and on she would go, every evening. Finally my wife had enough as said, "You know, this is all optional. If you don't like it, we can always pull you out." My wife went on to explain that hearing all of this whining was no fun for us, especially in light of everything the family was doing to make these lessons happen. Well our daughter's response was like night and day. After that every night we picked her up she would greet us with a huge smile and say she had a wonderful time. It warmed our hearts, and that's the payoff we were looking for. If we can't easily identify what our supporters are looking for then this may be a warning sign. We need to take the time to figure this out.

▶ **Mitigate the Impact:** People often resist change because it means more work for them. With time, energy, and cognitive resources all in limited supply, more work inevitably taxes our supporters' willingness to get behind us. Going back to the example of my daughter in dance classes, driving her all over creation and paying fees upon fees had a significant effect on our enthusiasm for this activity. One way we mitigated the impact (for ourselves—my daughter was too young to think about her supporters in this way) was by arranging carpools. Since these dance classes involved so much driving, carpooling even once or twice a week made a big difference.

▶ **Let Them Keep What They Love:** Another reason people might resist change is because they believe it will take something away that they value. If this is the case then we need to replace it with something they love. Otherwise what we're essentially asking them to do is to support us and lose something they love in return. That's a pretty hard sell. For example, years ago my wife decided she wanted to return to school and continue building her medical career. This was going to significantly curtail the time I got to spend with her—something I value a great deal. (I'm sort of codependent.) On the other hand, I knew how much she wanted this. Ever since she was young she wanted to work in the medical industry, and this was her chance to chase her dream. Of course I supported her plans, but something cool happened along the way. I became struck by how brilliantly she took to her classes, how neatly she established herself as the go-to person in the department, how effortlessly she picked up the art as well as the science of her vocation. And you know what? I fell in love with her all over again. I watched her in a state of awe and bragged about her any chance I got (such as right now). So in the end I had to give up something I loved— her company—but in return I got the satisfaction of seeing her pursue her dream and excel in the process. As far as I'm concerned I came out ahead. If you can't replace it with something they love then mitigate the impact of the loss. For example, maybe a family is working on getting out of debt, but also enjoys Friday night pizza. Getting pizza every Friday may cost too much, given the new goal of reducing debt, but maybe substitutes can be found. Frozen pizza, for instance, or a less expensive restaurant. Maybe instead of every Friday it's on payday Friday. Yes, this means it will take a little longer to get out of debt, but the family will remain onboard.

► **Warn Them of What Awaits if the Goal Is Not Reached, Again, Through Their Eyes:** In theory we change things because the status quo is no longer sufficient and there's an opportunity to improve. This means there's a benefit on the other side of change, one that improves upon the current state. True, change comes at a cost, but sometimes failure to change comes at a greater cost. For change to make sense the opportunity—minus the cost of change—must be greater than the risk of not changing—plus the cost not spent in making the change.

If we don't lose anything by maintaining the status quo then we're going to have a hard time creating a sense of urgency—a necessary ingredient in managing any change.

In Summary

1. **Know your supporters:** A supporter is anyone with a vested interest in your success.

2. **Engaged supporters amplifies what you can achieve:** What you can accomplish alone pales in comparison to what you can accomplish with the support of others.

3. **Accepting vs. embracing change:** Accepting change is passive, whereas embracing change means squeezing every ounce of benefit from it we can.

Your Turn

Go back to your notes from chapter four and review what you wrote about your supporters. There you answered such questions as:

▶ Who have been your supporters in the past?

▶ How has their support meant the difference between success and failure?

▶ What do these people hope to receive in return for their support?

▶ On the other side of the equation, who are your naysayers—those who have sought to discourage you?

With this in mind, think about what you'll need to do to keep your supporters actively engaged:

▶ What's the benefit of what you're trying to accomplish in their eyes?

_____

_____

_____

_____

_____

_____

_____

_____

▶ What might they have to give up to support you, and how can you mitigate that loss?

_____

_____

_____

_____

_____

_____

_____

► What will they be loath to give up if asked?

_____

_____

_____

_____

_____

_____

_____

_____

► How will it negatively affect them should they choose to hold back their support for your goals?

_____

_____

_____

_____

_____

_____

_____

_____

Remember, you want them to not merely accept any changes but to fully embrace them.

4. ABANDON THE MYTH OF MULTITASKING

Multitasking is the myth that refuses to die. We're seduced by its false promise of increased productivity. However, the research on multitasking is pretty clear.

Multitasking is a lie.

– Gary Keller

The first misconception about multitasking is that we're even multitasking in the first place. It's one thing to walk and chew gum at the same time; these are low-function tasks that require little in the way of cognitive resources. It's quite another to write a report, watch TV, surf Facebook, and text at the same time. The truth is we're not so much multitasking as we are task-switching. Still, numerous studies have demonstrated that switching from one task to another takes time and increases the chances of introducing errors.[1] Furthermore, the more complicated or unfamiliar the tasks, the greater the inefficiencies.[2] Not only does the mind need to shift from an existing task—one in which it has found its groove—to a new and unfamiliar task, but it also needs to remember where it was in the previous task, as well as where it moved into the new task.[3]

Also, the very act of switching tasks is a task in and of itself. This means we're committing precious cognitive resources to something that provides no value. Switching back and forth from multiple complex activities eradicates any efficiencies we hoped to gain by multitasking. Want numbers? Meyer and Kieras estimate that switching from task to task can result in a 40 percent drop in productivity.[4, 5] I don't know about you, but 40 percent of anything sounds like a lot to me.

Okay, so that's task-switching, but what about actual multitasking—instances where we're doing two things at once? Take, for instance, driving and talking on the phone. Researchers at the University of Utah found that motorists who talk on handheld or hands-free cellular phones are as impaired as drunken drivers.[6] What's more, these drivers took longer to reach their destinations when they chatted on cell phones than those who were simply talking with passengers.[7] The irony here is we think we're saving time by multitasking, but in truth it's slowing us down. Multitasking can also negatively affect our ability to collect and retain information. In a study performed in a university classroom, one group of students was allowed to use their laptops during the lecture, while a second group was asked to keep their laptops closed. As it turns out, students in the open laptop group struggled to remember the lecture content when compared to the closed laptop group.[8] Yet today's classrooms often encourage the use of electronic devices! Multitasking can also increase our sense of anxiety. Researchers out of University of California Irvine, found that people who received a steady stream of emails stayed in a perpetual "high alert" mode with higher heart rates than those without constant access to office email.[9]

Finally, multitaskers are awful at filtering out irrelevant distractions.[10] This means that while we may think we're focusing on two or three tasks at a time, we're really swimming in a soup of perpetual distraction. As Clifford Nass, a researcher from Stanford University puts it, "It turns out that high multitaskers are suckers for irrelevancy."[11]

So if multitasking is so bad, why is it so revered? The truth is that while multitasking is making us less productive, we're convinced it's doing just the opposite.[12] Even the researchers who conducted these studies on multitasking were surprised with the results. As Nass puts it, "It was a complete and total shock to me... [I] was sure [multitaskers] had some secret ability. But it turns out...multitaskers [are] just lousy at everything."[13]

At the end of the day the truth is this: multitasking doesn't enable us to do more in less time; it causes us to do less in more time.

Get in the Zone

Multitasking prevents us from getting in the zone—that amazing place where everything clicks and time seems to evaporate. Psychologists refer to being in the zone as *flow*. It's the full and complete engagement in a given task or activity to the exclusion of all else. Flow allows us to train our considerable cognitive resources on a task with the power of a laser beam.[14] Nothing stands a chance under that kind of attention. You know the feeling; it's extraordinary. So why we trade the stress and inefficiency of multitasking for the serendipitous experience of flow is beyond me. So abandon the myth of multitasking and enjoy the meditative state that comes with losing one's self in the task.

In Summary

1. **Multitasking is a myth:** Accept this and perform with intent; reject it and relegate your performance to lukewarm mediocrity.

2. **Get in the zone:** Multitasking prevents you from achieving flow—that amazing place where everything clicks and time seems to evaporate.

Your Turn

What's your take on multitasking? Are you focused on what you're doing, or are you doing several things at once, constantly switching your attention from one activity to another? If you're in this latter camp you may be skeptical that multitasking isn't the panacea of productivity we've all been told it is. Let's explore this a bit by answering these questions:

▶ Have you ever been so engrossed in an activity that you lost track of time? Why do you think that was? How did it feel?

_____

_____

_____

_____

_____

_____

_____

_____

▶ When you see someone texting and driving, or maybe checking messages during a movie, what do you think about that person? Are you comfortable with everyone thinking that about you if it were you doing it?

_____

_____

_____

_____

_____

_____

▶ When you multitask, how do you feel? Focused and sharp, or anxious and frazzled? Are you in the zone?

_____

_____

_____

_____

_____

_____

_____

▶ Have you ever seen a world-class athlete multitasking during a competition? No? Why do you think that is?

_____

_____

_____

_____

_____

_____

_____

If you're still not convinced then I'd like to issue this challenge: avoid all multitasking for two weeks and see how it turns out. It's going to be tough; I get that. I maintain that multitasking isn't _like_ a drug; it _is_ a drug. But gut through it for a couple weeks and see if your sense of focus, calm, and productivity doesn't improve. Remember, you want to be in the zone—in the _flow_.

5. STRIVE FOR PROGRESS; NOT PERFECTION

What is *perfect*? Is it a descriptor of quality? Affordability? Artistic merit? Refinement? Timeliness? Safety? Excitement? Utility? Scalability? It all depends on whom we ask and what's

> **Have no fear of perfection – you'll never reach it.**
>
> *– Salvador Dali*

important to them. Even if by some miracle we could come to an agreement on what perfect is, could we ever really achieve it? Something is perfect only as it relates to its environment, yet the environment is always changing. Just as in you can't step in the same river twice, the conditions that define something as perfect are ever-changing. Something that was perfect yesterday (pretending for a movement that such a thing were even possible) may be sub-par today.

Perfect is a meaningless term, yet somehow it has ensconced itself into our collective psyche as the gold standard in all we do. It's time to let go of this ridiculous expectation and focus instead on moving the ball down the field.

Progress Doesn't Have to Be Perfect to Be Effective

When a football team takes to the field, they don't concern themselves with perfect form, perfect coordination, perfect positioning, and perfect strategy. All they're concerned about is moving the ball down the field and making the touchdown. They want to perform to the best of their ability, to be sure, but what matters is not the performance but the outcome of that performance. In the same way, concerning ourselves with perfection misses the point. The only thing that matters is that we reach our goals in a way that's consistent with our guiding principles and North Star. How perfectly we do this is irrelevant.

Perfectionism Brings on Anxiety and Stress

Perfectionism can create and prolong a sense of anxiety and stress in our lives. It predisposes us to a low sense of life satisfaction and a feeling of hopelessness, even to the point of brining on depression and thoughts of suicide.[1, 2, 3] A good friend of mine is all too familiar with the costs associated with perfectionism. Early in his career he placed absurd expectations of perfection upon himself. This propensity came very naturally to him. Born the first of twelve children, he took the responsibility of oldest sibling very seriously. He came to believe that all the problems he saw were his alone to solve. This meant feeling accountable for anything and everything that happened in the family, including shielding his younger siblings from responsibility and taking everything on his shoulders. Adding to his consternation was my friend's analytical and hyper-detail-oriented nature. He was very meticulous and accurate in all that he did, to a fanatical degree. It may have taken him longer than most to complete a task, but in the end the outcome was excellent. Beyond excellent; it was *perfect*. Eventually however this need for perfection caught up with him. With all these unrealistic expectations on his shoulders, my friend became utterly overwhelmed. He was always exhausted yet couldn't sleep. Something was happening, and he wasn't sure what it was. As it turns out, he was having a nervous breakdown. The pressure he had placed upon himself to be perfect in everything he did had finally taken its toll. He was placed in a hospital for two months where he was treated for anxiety and depression. The good news is the treatment was successful and he emerged better able to cope with the stresses of work and his various responsibilities. From that time forward, my friend adopted the adage "progress; not perfection."

Insisting on Perfection Denies Us Our Wins

If the only result that matters is a perfect outcome then we'll never succeed. This means we'll never appreciate the progress we've made or the lessons we've learned along the way. We should allow ourselves to enjoy the small steps forward, the tiny triumphs, including the lessons we learn from our failures. Remember, two steps forward and one step back still comes out to one step forward. One step counts as progress. As track star Kim Collins is said to have remarked, "Strive for continuous improvement instead of perfection."

In Summary

1. **Progress doesn't have to be perfect to be effective:** The goal is to move the ball down the field. Do that enough times and you'll win the game.

2. **Perfectionism creates anxiety:** Perfectionism can create and prolong a sense of anxiety and stress. It predisposes you to a low sense of life satisfaction and a feeling of hopelessness, even to the point of brining on depression and thoughts of suicide.

3. **Insisting on perfection denies you your wins:** Perfectionism prevents you from appreciating the progress you've made or the lessons you've learned along the way.

Your Turn

It stands to reason that we should want to perform with a high level of quality, but quality is always balanced with resources such as cost and time. Insisting on perfection is not only impractical, it's impossible. With this in mind, do you ever find yourself hampered by perfectionism? If so, here are some things you may want to ponder:

▶ Why is it so important to you to be perfect?

_____

_____

_____

_____

_____

_____

_____

▶ How do you define perfection for yourself? Is that level of performance possible, given the resource requirements—time, money, support, energy, and so forth?

_____

_____

_____

_____

_____

_____

_____

▶ What has this need for perfection cost you in the past?

_____

_____

_____

_____

_____

_____

_____

_____

▶ How has your quest for perfection made you feel about yourself or your ability to perform?

_____

_____

_____

_____

_____

_____

_____

_____

To be sure, there's nothing wrong with striving for quality, but if it gets in the way of making measureable progress toward your Destination then you may be slipping into perfectionism. This can be problematic, so stay alert.

6. EMBRACE THE SERENITY PRAYER

The Serenity Prayer is likely one of the most famous prayers of modern times; probably the only verse to rival the Lord's Prayer.[1] Yet for all its fame, no one is entirely certain who penned the now-famous words. But while no one knows exactly where it came from, without a doubt the poem was made most famous by Reinhold Niebuhr and *Alcoholics Anonymous*. This organization used the poem to help its members keep perspective along their journey to sobriety. The poem (in part) reads as follows:

> **The greatest weapon against stress is our ability to choose one thought over another.**
>
> – *William James*

> *God grant me the serenity*
>
> *to accept the things I cannot change;*
>
> *courage to change the things I can;*
>
> *and wisdom to know the difference.*

There's another poem, less celebrated than the Serenity Prayer. However, in this case the author is known to many around the world. Mother Goose wrote:

> *For every ailment under the sun*
>
> *There is a remedy, or there is none;*
>
> *If there be one, try to find it;*
>
> *If there be none, never mind it.*

Both poems teach the same important principle: that we shouldn't worry ourselves over things we cannot control, but that we need to find the courage and wisdom to change the things we can.

Change the Person in the Mirror

Part of the Serenity Pray is knowing the difference between the things we cannot change and those we can, as well as the courage to change that which we must. This is significant because almost without fail the things we can change reside within ourselves. The problem is we tend to project the source of our problems on the external environment, like the decisions or behaviors of others. We tell ourselves that we would have been so much more successful if it hadn't of been for those things perpetrated upon our person by those around us—parents, bosses, spouses, children, governments, etc. Psychologists call this our *locus of control.* If we believe the outcomes of our actions are contingent on what we do, we have an internal-oriented locus of control. On the other hand, if we feel the outcomes are dependent on things outside our control then our locus of control is externally-oriented.[2]

When I was a small boy my father confronted me about something I had done. I can't remember what it was; probably something bad. Nor can I remember what I said to him, but it must have been something along the lines of, "It's not my fault." As I say, I don't remember any of this. What I do remember is what he said in response:

"Lon, no matter what happens, it's always your fault."

I don't know why but those words seared themselves into my skull. The phrase became my mantra. Whenever something happened and I felt the victim, my father's words would always return to me. "Lon, no matter what happens, it's always your fault." They caused me think about what I could have done differently, how I could have responded in the events leading up to a given incident. How maybe I could do things differently should I ever encounter that situation again.

Fast forward 15 years. I'm out driving with my then girlfriend (today my wonderful wife Susan) and I realize I'm barreling down on a line of cars barely moving forward in a traffic jam. I slam on the brakes and brace myself for the worse. By some miracle I come to a stop inches from the rear bumper of the car in front of me. (That driver would later tell me he was watching me in his rear-view mirror and figured this would be the end of him.)

The car came to a halt without incident and I breathed a sigh of relief.

Then our car exploded forward with a terrific crash.

I may have stopped inches from the car in front of us, but the car behind us wasn't so lucky. It stopped about three feet into our truck.

Later my girlfriend's father told me that it wasn't my fault. His opinion mattered in this situation. You see, it was his car I was driving.

And this was our first time meeting.

Not ideal.

Still, I couldn't shake the knowledge that it *was* my fault. Had I not been going so fast. Had I hit the brakes sooner. Had I looked in the rear-view mirror and gotten out of the way. There were any number of things I could have done to avoid that accident, regardless of who got the citation (the other guy, the poor kid). So today, when I have to stop short, what do I do? You better believe I look in my rear-view mirror and scan for an escape route in case something goes wrong.

Turn Your Locus of Control Inward

Those with an external locus of control tend to exhibit the following:

▶ Blame outside forces for their less-than desirable circumstances.

▶ Don't believe they can change their challenging circumstances through their own efforts.

▶ Frequently feel hopeless or powerless in the face of difficult challenges.

▶ Are more prone to experiencing a sense of helplessness.

Those with an internal locus of control tend to exhibit the following:

▶ Are more likely to take responsibility for their actions.

▶ Are less influenced by the opinions of others.

▶ Do well when allowed to work at their own pace.

▶ Have a strong sense of self-efficacy.

▶ Work hard to achieve the things they want.

▶ Feel confident in the face of challenges.

▶ Report being happier.

▶ Often achieve greater success.[3]

With this as our compass, it's not hard to see how the ADEPT Model and performing with intent flourishes with an internal locus of control. These folks are more likely to be entrepreneurial and find success in their endeavors.[4]

Let Go of False Conditions

Remember when you were a kid and you asked your parents a question? As often as not the answer was, "Because." Today we know what they meant: it's the way it is because it's the way it is. It's not open for debate, subject to interpretation, or eligible for amelioration. It's simply the way things are. In other words, "Because."

Some things in life simply are, and there's nothing we can do about it. I call these circumstances *environmental constants*. For example, water is wet. That's its state and nature. One can wish water were not quite so wet, but doing so would be futile. It's an environmental constant. Why is water wet? Because.

When we insist that an environmental constant has to change before we can feel a sense of satisfaction, purpose, or meaning, we're insisting on conditions that are unattainable, or as I call them, *false conditions*. A false condition is an environmental state that we perceive as necessary for our success but which cannot exist. In other words, it is something which we tell ourselves we need to be successful, but which is impossible to attain. For example, for a fish, his false condition would be insisting that he can only be happy once water is not so wet. For Sisyphus, his false condition was believing he needed to roll the stone to the top of the hill before he could feel a sense of accomplishment and purpose. But these things will never happen. For Sisyphus, his environmental constant ensures that the stone will always roll back down just before reaching the top. Insisting that happiness can only come from reaching the summit is a false condition.

Here are three types of false conditions we should be wary of:

1. The World Needs to Change for Us to Be Successful

As we mentioned before, water is wet. That's its nature, and for the most part that's not a problem. Fish do quite well in wet water. A fish doesn't complain that water is wet. If it did it would live a very frustrated and miserable existence. Even if it wanted to—even if it dedicated its every waking moment to the endeavor—a fish can never change the nature of wet water. It's an environmental constant. All a fish can hope to do is adapt to water's wet nature and live in harmony with its environment.

Like fish, we live in many environmental constants that cannot be changed. But unlike fish, we sometimes get it into our heads that these constants can and must be changed. We even convince ourselves that we won't be happy until they bend to our will. As a result we embark on a frustrating and ultimately futile journey as we try to change our environmental constants. We try to make water not wet.

We see this kind of behavior all the time. One time my son started a new job. He was nineteen but wasn't quite ready to head off to college, so he had few options available to him in terms of the sort of work he could choose. He ended up taking a job with a fast food joint in the local mall. His first week was hard, he told me, mostly because his boss had a thick accent that was difficult to understand. He told me how much easier his job would be and how much more he would enjoy it if his boss could just speak English. I agreed, but pointed out that the chances of this person developing fluent English devoid of any accent over the next few days for his benefit was not very likely, so it might be better if he were to drop this as a requirement for enjoying his new position.

We think about how much better it would be if our managers practiced better decision-making, if we had more time to complete a project, if our co-workers were better team players, if our bonuses better reflected our individual accomplishments, if there wasn't such favoritism in the workplace, and so on. Granted, these can all be very frustrating and at times make us want to scream, but in most cases they're environmental constants and not likely to change any time soon. At the very least they're classic examples of an external locus of control. Making our happiness contingent on these sorts of things is a false condition.

On the other hand...

Mind you, just because something is about as close to wet water as one can get doesn't mean it may not need changing, and that you may not be the person to change it. If a cause gives you meaning and purpose then social barriers—no matter how formidable—shouldn't throw you off course when others say it's impossible. For example, in 1983 Harvard Law student Evan Wolfson wrote a paper entitled *Same-sex marriage and morality: The human rights vision of the constitution.*

He got a B.

Despite his grade, that paper would later become known as the blueprint for the same-sex marriage movement. Just over 30 years later, Wolfson's *Freedom to Marry* organization would see same-sex marriage legalized in the US.[5] No doubt many would have considered his cause an example of fighting an environmental constant, yet he stuck with it.

Recently a relative of mine asked the family to refer to them in gender-neutral terms. Instead of "him" or "her," they asked that we refer to them as "them" or "they," saying they felt more plural than singular anyway. On the surface this seems like a classic case of wet water—insisting that an environmental constant change to meet one's own particular preference. While this person may not identify with any specific gender and feel more plural than singular, the fact is that from the day we were born we perceive individuals and genders. However, by this same argument blacks shouldn't have bothered fighting slavery, women should have given up all hope of one day voting, and the LGBTQ community should have abandoned any thought of one day seeing same-sex marriage legalized. All these causes fought against social practices that were so entrenched that they could have easily been categorized as environmental constants. The gender-neutral movement is in many very similar. Currently there's a growing gender-neutral pronoun movement underway in many countries. For instance, in Sweden an effort is underway to introduce the gender-neutral pronoun "hen" into the national vocabulary.[6] Recently Sweden updated their dictionary to include this pronoun.[7] As stated in the Serenity Prayer, the key is knowing the difference between an environmental constant that should be accepted and an inspiring cause that should be courageously pursued.

2. Everything Is Either Good or Bad

When I was young and learning French I was completely perplexed by the notion that objects had genders. A fork is feminine, but a knife is masculine. A car is feminine; a bicycle is masculine. Cup, feminine; glass, masculine. Everything had a gender. It drove me nuts!

"We have a tendency to assign moral values to things that are amoral. Shakespeare's Hamlet once said, 'There is nothing either good or bad, but thinking makes it so.'"

I complained constantly that this was ridiculous and that French would be so much easier to learn if it were to drop this nonsense. (Talk about an environmental constant and a false condition! I'm sure the French people would have been only too happy to change their language for my benefit.)

We do the same thing; not with genders but with value judgments. We have a tendency to assign moral values to things that are amoral. Shakespeare's Hamlet once said, "There is nothing either good or bad, but thinking makes it so." How right he was. We often talk in terms "good" weather or "bad" weather when really there's no such thing as either; there's only weather. Our perception of the weather is dependent on what we want to do in it. Windy weather is great for sailing but awful for cycling.

The problem with attaching a moral value to an environmental constant is it imposes the idea of right and wrong on something that is separate from morality, but which in turn feeds our desire to change or fight that which we perceive as wrong. Imagine how much more miserable the fish would be if he decided that not only was wet water physically uncomfortable but morally wrong as well! This is often the root of culture shock—the idea that what we do is right, therefore what someone else does is by definition wrong. I'm not saying some conditions are not more preferable than others, but saying it's wrong that you should have to wait three minutes for an elevator, for example, is a false condition. There is nothing wrong with three minutes, and insisting that there is doesn't make it so.

3. Sense of Expectation and Entitlement

There's an annual event in my area called the *Salt Lake Parade of Homes*. It's a chance for local builders to show off the latest in home innovations, styles, decorations, and designs. Inevitably the homes are grand on an insane scale, or so I'm told. You see, I've never gone to a showcase home, and here's why: I love my home. I love where I live. I feel very blessed to be where I am. This being the case, why would I want to walk through home after home, all sending me the same message: you miserable sod; you live in a hovel? Michael J. Fox is purported to have once said, "My happiness grows in direct proportion to my acceptance, and in inverse proportion to my expectations." I'm very happy to accept where I live. Viewing model homes would do nothing but raise my expectations and devalue what I have. No thanks.

Consider this scenario: we go out to our car one morning, turn the key, and the engine starts. What do we feel? Probably not a whole lot. It's what we expected when we turned the key. It's not like the thing just turned water into wine or anything. Besides, purchasing the car entitles us to a vehicle that performs as the manufactured promised.

Now imagine we go out to our car one cold morning, turn the key, and hear a roar, a sputter, followed by a loud bang, then silence. Now what do we feel? Annoyance? Frustration? Dread at the thought of how much this is going to cost to fix?

Whatever our feelings, chances are they're rooted in our sense of expectation and entitlement. Perhaps no other perceptions are as poisonous to our sense of fulfillment as are expectation and entitlement. They're the feelings that tell us we're not happy with what we have, that we should have more, that we deserve better. These perceptions tell us we should have a bigger office, a nicer car, a larger home, a skinnier waist, and a fatter bonus. When expectation and entitlement rule, they cause us to be unsatisfied with our current circumstance. This can give power to our false conditions and make us miserable.

The opposite of expectation is gratitude. Whereas expectation magnifies the gap between what we have and what we feel we aught have to be happy, gratitude focuses our attention on how rich we truly are as a result of what we already have.

In Summary

1. **Accept the things you cannot change:** The world doesn't need to change for you to be successful; you need to change.

2. **Turn your locus of control inward:** Those with an internal locus of control are more likely to be successful in their endeavors.

3. **Let go of your false conditions:** Don't make your success contingent on something you cannot change.

Your Turn

Do you ever find yourself saying to yourself, "If only these conditions were different, *then* I could be successful," or something along those lines? If you can do something about these circumstances then you should. If, on the other hand, these things are outside your influence then they're false conditions. Let's explore this idea:

▶ What sort of false conditions might be preventing you from moving forward? For example, have you ever said, "If only the economy were better, then I could be successful?" No argument here, but can you change the economy? To me, this is classic wet water.

_____

_____

_____

_____

_____

_____

_____

_____

▶ Do you sometimes feel like you're being pushed around by things outside your control? If so, what might these forces look like? You may not be able to remove them, but can you mitigate their effects? Reduce their power over you?

_____

_____

_____

_____

_____

_____

_____

▶ Do you know what needs to be done, but then find yourself making excuses as to why you can't do it? For example, if you need to return to school, what's stopping you? Are there true obstacles in your way, or are you making up excuses to say it's out of your control?

_____

_____

_____

_____

_____

_____

_____

_____

▶ Have you had times when a sense of expectation or entitlement derailed your progress?

_____

_____

_____

_____

_____

_____

_____

At the end of the day this is all about taking the power from things outside your control and keeping it for yourself. After all, if it's outside your control, why give it power over you?

7. LEARN FROM YOUR FAILURES

Ugh. Failure.

It's that 'F' we got back in school that still haunts us. It's coming in last in that big race, that new job that kindly asked us to leave after three months with the firm, that business venture that tanked and took our credit rating with it, that marriage that seemed to fall

> Failure is, in a sense, the highway to success, inasmuch as every discovery of what is false leads us to seek earnestly after what is true, and every fresh experience points out some form of error which we shall afterwards carefully avoid.
>
> – *John Keats*

apart right before our very eyes. It's all the things we don't want to think about because they conjure such feelings of worthlessness, self-doubt, and…well… *failure*.

I hear ya'.

Still, it's something we need to overcome. Failure is a treasure chest full of knowledge and learning; the currency of tomorrow's success. Performing with intent requires that we constantly hone our intent, and failure is the stone against which we sharpen our blade.

Failure's Connection with Blame and Shame

One thing that prevents us from taking the time to internalize and learn from our failures is what Amy Edmondson calls the *blame game*. We learn the blame game and its emotional impact early on as children. When we do something wrong we're blamed, and with blame comes ridicule and shame. That emotional response follows us from childhood right into adulthood. Add to this the fact that many promotions and career opportunities can evaporate when we're blamed for some misstep and it's not hard to see why we don't want to associate ourselves with failure.[1] However, in allowing this blame and shame to ride on the coattails of failure we miss a tremendous opportunity to learn and improve.

Blameworthy vs. Praiseworthy Failure

Not all failure is created equal. It's generally desirable to avoid the sort of failure that comes from the deliberate violation of a standard principle or inattention to the task at hand. When a teen is texting while driving (deliberate violation of a standard principle—the law), is distracted (inattention to the task at hand),

and causes an accident, about the only lesson to be learned from this failure is to obey the law and pay attention. Edmondson would call this a *blameworthy* event. On the other hand, when we experiment and test ideas in an uncertain environment we can gather a great deal of valuable information from failure—information that will increase the odds of success in the future. In these cases the blame game makes no sense and can be extremely damaging to the process. Instead, Edmondson says we should regard this as a *praiseworthy* event.[2] Failure as praiseworthy? Absolutely, especially when it produces such valuable information. This principle is expressed beautifully in an interview with Thomas Edison back in 1921 in which he said:

> *"I never allow myself to become discouraged under any circumstances. I recall that after we had conducted thousands of experiments on a certain project without solving the problem, one of my associates, after we had conducted the crowning experiment and it had proved a failure, expressed discouragement and disgust over our having failed 'to find out anything.' I cheerily assured him that we had learned something. For we had learned for a certainty that the thing couldn't be done that way, and that we would have to try some other way."*[3]

A failure is only a failure if we learn nothing from it. So what can we do to ensure we learn from our missteps and keep moving forward? Here are four steps we can follow:

1. Detect Failure

Because failure is often associated with shame, it's tempting to overlook our mistakes. We generally strive to avoid failure, so it can be challenging to rally the emotional courage needed to take a good hard look at our fumbles. Avoidance, rather than detection, tends to be the name of the game. As Edmondson says, "Spotting big, painful, expensive failures is easy. But in many organizations any failure that can be hidden is hidden as long as it's unlikely to cause immediate or obvious harm. The goal should be to surface it early, before it has mushroomed into disaster."[4] We need to understand this natural tendency to overlook our failures and ferret out these gems wherever we can find them.

2. Accept Failure

Earlier we talked about the importance of establishing an internal locus of control. This introspective tendency will help us learn from our mistakes. According to a study at the Harvard Business School, taking personal ownership for an outcome will increase the likelihood that we'll learn from our mistakes and adjust our approach the next time around. Conversely, if it's unclear whether we're responsible for the failure, or if we place the blame outside of ourselves—externalizing it through the blame game— then it's unlikely we'll learn from anything meaningful the experience.[5] The goal therefore should be to own our failures and see them as an outcome of our own actions—not the actions of others.

3. Analyze Failure

Remember that failure is a treasure chest full of knowledge and learning; the currency of tomorrow's success. Who among us, upon opening a treasure chest full of gold, coins, jewels, and bobbles, wouldn't immediately begin examining, admiring, and inventorying the booty, all with an eye toward the possibilities this newfound wealth can provide? Wouldn't your heart jump, your pulse race, and your hands tremble with excitement? That's what we should be doing with our failures. According to Edmondson, "Once a failure has been detected, it's essential to go beyond the obvious and superficial reasons for it to understand the root causes. This requires the discipline—better yet, the enthusiasm—to use sophisticated analysis to ensure that the right lessons are learned and the right remedies are employed."[6] It's only by analyzing the failure that we can gain the value buried deep in the experience.

4. Modify Our Approach

We should take what we learn from our analysis and adjust how we approach a problem or a challenge. Einstein purportedly said the definition of insanity is doing the same thing over and over again and expecting different results. Analyzing and applying the lessons learned from our failures will be the key to avoiding that particular brand of insanity.

All of this means that, from a practical perspective, we need to dismiss the idea that failure is something shameful and catastrophic. Instead, we need to treat it as an opportunity to grow and succeed.[7]

Failure Motivates You to Succeed

In 2013 I was all set to participate in my fourth Ironman. I knew I wasn't in the best shape of my life, but I felt I was prepared enough to complete this thing without too much pain and suffering. Truth is, I was lying to myself. Over the years I had become complacent in my training and I was bored. Besides, I figured I had always succeed in the past; this time would be no different.

I probably don't have to tell you that it went poorly.

I'll spare you the gory details, but suffice it to say I had my first DNF (Did Not Finish). Before that day I had always said, "Better dead than DNF," but this race showed me the unmitigated hubris in this saying.

Well I didn't want this to be the way I ended my Ironman career, so I signed up for another race the following year. This time I was motivated. With the sting of failure fresh in my heart I took my training very seriously. Not a day went by in which I didn't recall the moment I abandoned the race and the shame I had felt. I used that as a motivation to work harder than I ever had before. What's more, I took all the lessons I learned from that failure and integrated them into my training program. In short, my failure became a blueprint for my future success. It turned me into a smart, hard-working, motivated athlete. And in August of 2014 I had the best Ironman of my life—all because of my embarrassing DNF.

Joshua Waitzkin, international chess master and subject of the 1993 film *Searching for Bobby Fischer* says this about failure:

> *"I think losing my first National Chess Championship was the greatest thing that ever happened to me, because it helped me avoid many of the psychological traps [of being a child prodigy]. That year, between ages eight and nine was one of the most formative periods of my life. I had felt my mortality, came back strong, and went on to dominate the scholastic chess scene over the next eight years. On some fundamental level, the notion of success in my being was defined by overcoming adversity—and it still is."*[8]

The chief psychological trap Josh overcame was the belief that he was special; that he didn't need to work hard, fail, get up, and work even harder to become a champion. As someone who demonstrated an incredible talent for chess very early on, it was probably very tempting for him to believe what everyone around him was saying; that he was a child prodigy. By losing his first championship he quickly learned that talent wasn't enough. He learned he had to work hard and fail from time to time.[9] As he put it, he had felt his mortality, and that was the impetus he need to apply himself at a whole new level.

In Summary

1. **Today's praiseworthy failure is the key to tomorrow's success:** Failure is a treasure chest full of knowledge and learning; the currency of tomorrow's success. Performing with intent requires that you constantly hone that intent, and failure is the stone against which you sharpen your blade.

Your Turn

This might sting a little, but it'll be worth it, I promise. Think back to some of the failures that have stood in the way of your progress. As you do, let's analyze them a bit and see what we can learn:

▶ Think of a painful, perhaps even humiliating failure in your past. How did it make you feel?

_____

_____

_____

_____

_____

_____

_____

▶ What sort of lessons did you learn from this?

_____

_____

_____

_____

_____

_____

_____

▶ How have these lessons benefited you since?

_____

_____

_____

_____

_____

_____

_____

_____

▶ What successes have you enjoyed that would not have been possible had it not been for your failures?

_____

_____

_____

_____

_____

_____

_____

_____

▶ Are there any failure you've come to look back upon fondly? What is it
   about these failures that's different from those you still regard with shame?

_____

_____

_____

_____

_____

_____

_____

_____

As you can see, it's all about recalibrating your attitude toward failure. Stop
looking at it as a badge of shame and embrace it as a necessary step that will get
you closer to winning the championship.

8. BEWARE OF OVERLOAD AND ANXIETY

I once worked with an executive who, as far as I could ascertain, had the singular life goal of one day spontaneously combusting in a Michael-Bay-esque explosion of frantic anxiety. Racing this way and that, his arms full of papers, a laptop, three cell phones, and

It can kind of screw up things if you're trying to overwork something.

– Jeff Bridges

technical manuals the size of the Gutenberg Bible; he was perpetually late to every meeting he ever attended, if not completely absent. He spoke a hundred miles an hour and with nervous energy. He could never be found or nailed down, always off to do this or that, here and there.

Yes, you might say, but was he *productive*? No doubt the likes of Steve Jobs and Elon Musk exhibited the same level of energy and anxiety, but they had a lot to show for their effort. This individual, I'm sorry to say, was not as successful in any of his endeavors. He was spread too thin, confusing *busy* with *productive.*

Now in reading this you may think I wasn't terribly fond of the man. Not so. In fact, I found myself almost magnetically drawn to him. He was charming and charismatic. I enjoyed his energy a great deal. The problem was he had allowed himself to become overloaded. He's not alone. As Hallowell aptly put it, "Frenzied executives who fidget through meetings, miss appointments, and jab at the elevator's 'door close' button aren't crazy—just crazed."[1]

Attention Deficit Trait

These people (and yes, sometimes we're included in this category of over-extended crazed individuals) suffer from a neurological phenomenon called *attention deficit trait* (ADT). The condition is characterized by distractibility, inner frenzy, and impatience. (Does this sound familiar at all?) It prevents us from clarifying our priorities, making sound decisions, and managing our time effectively. In essence, as Hallowell puts it, ADT turns otherwise talented performers into harried underachievers.[2]

ADT isn't an illness or some sort of character defect. It's our brain's natural response to the ever-expanding demands placed upon it. As our brains are bombarded with more and more information, our cognitive resources are over-taxed and we lose the ability to perform. Our creativity goes out the window, our capacity to handle ambiguity evaporates, and soon we're making more mistakes than we can count. However, because it's simply a natural response to our hyperkinetic environment, we can take steps to mitigate the effects. Here are some things we can do to combat ADT:

▶ **Monitor Your Self-Talk:** It has to be some weird kind of irony that the most critical person in the room is often ourselves. Here we are, anxious about getting the work done, dealing with multiple streams of information, and engaging with others, all the while sabotaging our own performance with fear and self-doubt. Negative emotions such as these can throw the brakes on any hope of productivity. I frequently find myself thinking things like, "I'm going to say something stupid and come off as an ass," "Everyone else in the room is smarter and more successful than I," "They're all going to see that I'm a fake," and, "I have no idea what I'm going to say to these people." Stow that nonsense. Stow it, and replace it with positive affirmations. Tell yourself that, actually, you're pretty darn sharp, have been known to be charming on occasion, and have a lot to offer.

▶ **Get a Good Night's Sleep:** When we lose sleep we lose the ability to think on our feet, take in new information, and adjust our behavior.[3] In one study researchers rounded up a bunch of volunteers; half went without any sleep for two days; the other half slept normal hours. Over the course of a week the researchers tested everyone's ability to complete decision-making tests. In one test the volunteers had to click a button when they saw certain numbers and hold back when they saw others. Then the rules were switched. In general the well-rested group did better than the sleep-deprived group, but when the rules were reversed none of the sleep-deprived volunteers were able to get the right answer—at all—even after 40 tries! "It wasn't just that sleep-deprived people were slower to recover," said Paul Whitney, a psychologist who led the study. "Their ability to take in new information and adjust was completely devastated."[4] Sleep well each night and avoid this trap.

▶ **Take Frequent Breaks:** Boxers can't wail on each other indefinitely. They need breaks. To keep sharp, every three minutes they go to their respective corners, rest, take stock, and gather themselves for the next round. We can do the same thing. We can leave the environment for a minute or two and allow ourselves the chance to take a breather and bring our anxiety into check. Remember that prolonged sedentary time can have a negative effect on our health and depletes our cognitive resources.[5] Taking short breaks recharges these resources and makes us more productive.[6]

Physical activity has also been widely associated with enhanced cognitive processing.[7] In other words, getting out clears the head. With this in mind, consider getting outside and taking a walk. Taking a break and visiting green spaces can have a restorative effect, improving attention fatigue and quickening stress recovery.[8]

▶ **OHIO (Only Handle It Once):** Each time we deal with a document, email, voicemail, or some other task, we should do whatever needs to be done then move on. The more times we handle something, the less efficient we become. In fact, by handling something multiple times we only succeed in creating more work from less. Who wants *that*? Consider this all-too-familiar scenario: we receive an email, read it, then decide to deal with it later. A day or two passes and we forget what that email said so we reread it. Still though we leave it in our "to-do" pile. A couple days later we receive a reminder from whoever sent us the email in the first place. We read the reminder, then go back and reread the original a third time. Hopefully by now we've learned our lesson and close out the original request. If not, the cycle of spontaneous work creation continues. Had we just dealt with the email the first time we wouldn't have had to process all the extra work we created for ourselves. So do the task and be done with it. Be draconian about moving things off the docket.

Make Stress Your Ally

When you think about stress, what comes to mind? Trouble sleeping? Headaches? Blood pressure? Stomach problems? Chest pain? This shouldn't be any surprise; these are all documented effects of stress on our heath.[8] Thing is, they don't need to be. Stanford University psychologist Kelly McGonigal found something interesting, which is this: stress is bad for your health—if, that is, you *think* stress is bad for your health.[10] (That's right; go ahead and reread that sentence. I'll wait.) What McGonigal found was the way we think about stress changes how it affects our health. As she put it, "When you change your mind about stress you can change your body's response to stress."[11] Here's the way it works: when we're confronted with a stressful situation we break out into a sweat, we breathe faster, and our heart rate increases. Now, we can associate these physiological responses with anxiety and signs that we're not coping well with the pressure—things that are slowly sending us to the grave—or we can choose to see them as ways our bodies are becoming energized, preparing to meet the challenge before us and knock it out of the park. McGonigal found that those who chose to view stress as something to help prepare them (rather than kill them) actually benefit from the stress response.[11]

We can learn from this and rethink how we view stress in our lives. Now I'm not saying we should go off and actively seek out copious stress and anxiety, but at least we can embrace it when it does come along. Look at it not as the Grim Reaper but as a coach firing us up before the big game.

In Summary

1. **Monitor your self-talk:** Remind yourself that you rock and you've got this.

2. **Get a good night's sleep:** Sleep deprivation devastates your ability to perform, so get that shuteye.

3. **Take breaks:** Taking short breaks makes you more productive.

4. **Be draconian about moving tasks off your plate:** Do the task and be done with it. Don't create extra work for yourself.

5. **Embrace stress:** Think of stress as your body's way of preparing you to meet the challenge.

Your Turn

Everyone feels stress and anxiety from time to time. It's what keeps you sharp and focused. It's going to happen, so the only question is how are you going to respond to it. With that in mind, consider the following:

▶ How do you know when you're overloaded? How do you feel mentally, emotionally, and physically?

_____

_____

_____

_____

_____

_____

_____

_____

▶ How do you think this affects your performance?

_____

_____

_____

_____

_____

_____

_____

_____

▶ What are some of the ways you cope with stress and anxiety? What seems to work best for you?

_____

_____

_____

_____

_____

_____

_____

_____

▶ What other things might you try to reduce the feeling of being overloaded?

_____

_____

_____

_____

_____

_____

_____

_____

The goal is to develop a calm serenity in which you can focus your efforts and perform to your fullest potential without distraction. Stress and anxiety are going to be persistent partners, but you can make sure they don't run the show.

9. KEEP IT ALL IN PERSPECTIVE

For years I managed a team for a global high-tech manufacturing company. One of my duties was delivering annual performance reviews to my employees. This particular year I had the opportunity to review an employee who had had a phenomenal year. During a mid-year

> **Everything we hear is an opinion, not a fact. Everything we see is a perspective, not the truth.**
>
> – *Marcus Aurelius*

review a few months earlier the employee had been recognized and given a mid-year promotion (something not often done) and a ranking of "Outstanding" in the corporate parlance. With this rare mid-year promotion came a double-digit raise, a handsome stock grant, and an increased bonus percentage. Of course with a promotion came increased job responsibilities and expectations, but this too was something the employee had sought after.

This upcoming annual performance review was going to include much of the same. The employee had successfully met the increased job expectations and so was going to get small raise, a few more shares, and a performance ranking of "Successful." Granted, "Successful" was less than "Outstanding," but since the pay grade, responsibilities, and job expectations had increased, so had the bar. This was well understood in the corporate culture so I wasn't concerned.

I probably don't have to tell you things didn't go as I had anticipated. At first the review went well enough. I went over the employee's accomplishments, discussed his contributions, and offered some ideas on how he might continue to increase his value to the company. Then I delivered the performance summary. I told the employee that he was receiving a performance ranking of "Successful" and itemized his additional raise and stock grant. To my surprise the employee's expression fell. As far as he was concerned he had just been given a letter grade of "C" for the year. I tried to explain that having been promoted to a new pay grade a few months previous the expectations had increased, but none of this seemed to matter. He felt let down. Then he said something that really struck me.

"We give so much of ourselves to our jobs, it's hard not to take this as a review of my life."

This employee had made his sense of self-worth as a person contingent on one word: "Successful."

Contingencies of Self-Worth

The things that give us meaning and purpose can become what are known as *contingencies of self-worth*. As the term suggests, it means making our personal sense of self-worth contingent on something outside ourselves,[1] like the outcome of a performance review. It's the opposite of what Sisyphus, Frankl, and Dennis taught us earlier. Rather than deciding for ourselves how we measure our worth, we let others decide for us.

The workplace can be an especially dangerous place when it comes to contingencies of self-worth. Many things in life give us purpose and meaning, but most are hard to quantify and compare. How do we quantify our performance as parents, spouses, or friends? On the other hand, our society makes it easy to quantify and compare our performance as employees. It's call *salary* and *job title*. With these supreme metrics in hand we can cut and slice the world and see where we fit in the community. Considering how much time and energy we dedicate to the workplace, it's no wonder it accounts for such a large portion of our view of ourselves. This can be dangerous to our overall wellbeing. Keeping things in perspective can help shield us from this danger.

Just Because It's Important to You Doesn't Mean It's Important

Be careful you don't drink your own Kool-Aid. Purpose and meaning, directed by clear and focused intent, is a very powerful thing. It has built nations, sent humankind to the stars, eradicated deadly diseases, created magnificent works of art, and inspired spiritual unity. With all this in mind, it may not be hard to imagine that sometimes we get a little carried away. We start to think that everything—not only our lives but the lives of those around us—should be dedicated to fulfilling this purpose. This can be a problem. Everyone is inspired by his or her own meaning and purpose, and just as no one can tell us what ours may be, we cannot dictate the purpose of others. Everyone gets to choose what's important to him or her, and it may so happen that what matters to us doesn't matter a hill of beans to someone else.

I frequently see this sort of biased perspective in the workplace. We get so caught up in the role we perform at work that we forget we're just a small part of the whole. Back when I worked for this tech company I mentioned earlier I attended a corporate communicators conference. In attendance were about 200 professional communicators from around the world, all responsible for communicating company information to the more than 80,000 employees; everything from corporate strategy to HR services. (Yep. That's a real job.)

One of the speakers at this conference was from the legal department. She gave her presentation (on what I can't remember) then opened the floor up for questions. Someone raised his hand and asked when should we engage with Legal for approval before sending a communication off to the employees. It was a question we all shared. Traditionally we just used our best judgment, but really what we wanted were clear criteria so we could better plan our projects and keep the company legally compliant.

We thought we'd hear something along those lines, but instead she told us that every single communication should pass through Legal. Now keep in mind, this group of 200 communicators sent out hundreds of communications every week. Some were videos and articles for the entire company; others were short emails targeting five or six employees. Some dealt with very sensitive information; others were little more than memos about when the parking lot was to be repainted and plans for kid-to-work day. The person asking the question pointed this out to help the speaker understand what he was looking for. Obviously, Legal didn't want to see *every single* communication, right? Wrong. Legal, she insisted, must review and approve every piece of information that's sent to the employees.

So what happened here? Why did the speaker insist that Legal had to review and approve everything? Because she was convinced of the all-important role of her function. For her, everything orbited around her role.

We all do this to some extent. Sales says that without them there would be no revenue and therefore no company. Marketing says that without them there would be no market demand and therefore no sales. Manufacturing says that without them there would be no product and therefore nothing to market or sell. Human Resources says that without them there would be no employees to manufacture the products to market or sell. The cycle goes on. We all like to think we're integral to the universe, and that's fine. It's a beautiful lie, one that emboldens us to give our very best to everything we do, no matter how trivial it may be. But sometimes we lose perspective and forget that's all it is: nothing more than a beautiful lie.

Pet Causes

In his Netflix TV special, *Thinky Pain*, comedian Marc Maron pokes some pretty relentless fun at people who seem to feel everyone should believe as they do when it comes to their pet causes. In particular, he zeros in on vegans and atheists. He goes on to say he'd rather spend an hour with a reasonable

Christian on a mission than spend any time at all with an atheist vegan.[2]

Now if you're an atheist or a vegan (or both), chances are you're feeling a tinge of resentment right about now. (Hey, I'm gluten-free and on my own metaphysical journey, so I feel ya'.) But that's sort of the point. Nothing's worse than having others try to decide what should or shouldn't be important to us, so don't be that person. Keep it in perspective. Live and let live.

In Summary

1. **Keep things in perspective:** Don't let any one thing factor in too much when deciding how you feel about yourself.

2. **It's not as important as you think it is:** Everything is important to someone; you don't have a monopoly on righteous causes. Be careful you don't start believing the beautiful lie; that your cause trumps all others.

3. **Don't try to decide for others what should or shouldn't be important:** We all get to decide this for ourselves.

THE COURAGE TO SUCCEED

Your Turn

When you give so much of yourself to your passions it can be easy to lose perspective. It helps to bear in mind that nothing—no matter how important something may be—should be allowed to completely define who you are or your value as a person. With that said, here are some things to ask yourself:

▶ Have you ever failed at something and been rocked to the core as a result? How did you eventually pick yourself back up?

_____

_____

_____

_____

_____

_____

_____

▶ How do you feel when other's don't share your passions, or even take them seriously at all?

_____

_____

_____

_____

_____

_____

_____

▶ How do you feel when others try to force their pet causes on you?

_____

_____

_____

_____

_____

_____

_____

_____

▶ How do you feel when others demean or belittle things that are important
to you?

_____

_____

_____

_____

_____

_____

_____

_____

THE COURAGE TO SUCCEED

▶ Are there beliefs or causes out there that you may have belittled in the past?

_____

_____

_____

_____

_____

_____

_____

_____

Don't forget what we talked about in chapter four: just because something *gives* you purpose and meaning doesn't mean that it *has* purpose and meaning. But that's okay. Meaning is in the eye of the beholder, and everything is important to someone. If it inspires you then fantastic. Just make sure you keep everything in perspective as you work toward your North Star.

10. ENJOY THE JOURNEY

My wife and I love family road trips. Now and again, when we're driving late at night along the highway, one of us will comment that the drive has a sort of "road trip" feel about it, which is to say it's comfortable, serene, quiet, devoid of stress and anxiety—all very pleasant.

> **Every day is a journey, and the journey itself is home.**
>
> – *Matsuo Basho*

Compare this with air travel—that grand social experiment designed to see how much pain and suffering a group of humans can endure before all vestiges of civilization are raked from their souls and the world descends into chaos. Sure, flying gets us there quicker, but for me, driving is infinitely more enjoyable. In fact, the drive is part of the vacation experience, whereas flying is a perfunctory requirement to get to where I want to go.

We embark on journeys because we see great potential, opportunity, and reward on the other side. However, this doesn't mean we can't enjoy the journey itself. Why tell ourselves, "I'll be happy when..." when we can be happy *now*?

The Journey Is the Destination

In his seminal work, *The Hero with a Thousand Faces*, Joseph Campbell describes what he calls a *monomyth*, or the hero's journey. Campbell demonstrates in great detail how many of the great myths and legends of the world follow a common arc. There's the departure, where our hero leaves behind the mundane life and is thrust into something great and perhaps even terrible. At first the hero might refuse the call, but then receives aid from a mentor. This gives the hero the courage to move forward. Next is the initiation. Here the hero must endure a series of tests, challenges, and ordeals that mold and transform him or her into something greater than before. Then come the final tests. These often include resisting the temptations of comfort and ease, or atonement with a father or some other authority figure. The trials concluded, the hero then embarks on the return voyage. Here the adventurer delivers the knowledge and treasures needed to help others strike off on their own journeys.[1]

If this sounds very familiar, it should. As Campbell states, just about every great story told follows this pattern. Even modern stories such as *Star Wars* follow this arc.[2, 3] It could also very well be that you've experienced such a journey yourself. The reason the pattern resonates with us is because it's familiar to our own life's journey.

I'm stressing the journey because in these stories it's the journey that's interesting, that fascinates, that educates, that builds our sense of self and our character. The ending of the story is almost a formality. In fact, if all we were interested in was the ending then we would read the last chapter of the book and show up to the movie in time to catch the last ten minutes. Endings are all well and good, but it's the journey that compels our attention.

As we implement the ADEPT Model, we're embarking upon an incredible journey. We should revel in the process. Treat the journey as a fulfilling accomplishment in and of itself. Enjoy the learning and the growth, the successes as well as the stumbles. We get on the rollercoaster to experience the ride; not to come to a jerking halt at the end.

In Summary

1. **The journey is the destination:** It's the journey that's interesting, that fascinates, that educates, that builds your sense of self and your character. Arriving at the destination is almost a formality.

Your Turn

Are you the sort of person who's in a hurry to get somewhere, or do you take pleasure in the journey? Here are some questions for you to consider:

▶   Think back to a family vacation or some similar excursion. What about the journey made it an adventure? One time I took a boat, a bus, a train, a plane, and a subway all in day. After a journey like that, arriving at my destination was almost anticlimactic!

_____

_____

_____

_____

_____

_____

_____

▶   What have you learned about yourself and others during a journey?

_____

_____

_____

_____

_____

_____

_____

► How soon after arriving at your destination do you start thinking of your next journey?

_____

_____

_____

_____

_____

_____

_____

_____

John Lennon once said that life is what happens when we're busy making plans. I'm hip, but I'd rephrase this and say that life is what happens when we're busy rushing from one destination to the next. Slow down and enjoy the journey. After all, the destination for all of us is the grave. Why be in such a hurry?

CHAPTER 8: CONCLUSION
(or rather, Beginning)

There are no secrets to success. It is the result of preparation, hard work, persistence, and learning from failure.

– Colin Powell
American statesman, general in the United States Army

I hope you find the material in this book helpful. While using these practices has made a tremendous difference in my own life, I'm keenly aware that not all sizes fit all. And you know what? That's totally fine. I invite you to pick and choose, select and discard, accept and reject from these principles and craft your own journey toward success. Ultimately that's all that matters: that you unlock the secret to your own potential and achieve amazing things.

So now it's time to stop reading and start performing with intent. As you do so, keep the ADEPT Model close to heart:

Accept	Accept the three economic laws of performing with intent.
Discover	Discover what matters most and gives you meaning and purpose.
Eliminate	Eliminate what doesn't matter—things that are distracting you from your purpose.
Plan	Plan a course of action to achieving what matters.
Take Action	Take action and develop the mindset you need to accomplish great things.

Finally, I'd like to leave you with a poem by Robert Frost:

Grant me intention, purpose and design –
That's near enough for me to the divine.

And yet with all this help of head and brain,
How happily instinctive we remain.
Our best guide upward farther to the light:
Passionate preference such as love at sight.

This may be the end of the book, but it's the beginning of your journey. I'm excited to hear what you accomplish!

REFERENCES

INTRODUCTION

1. Drucker, P. F. (1954). *The practice of management.* New York, NY: Harper & Row.

CHAPTER 1: BEWARE

1. Bruch, H., & Ghoshal, S. (2002). Beware the busy manager. *Harvard Business Review, 80*(2), 62-69.

2. Covey, S. M. R., & Merrill, R. R. (2006). *The speed of trust: The one thing that changes everything.* New York, NY: Free Press.

3. Gavin, J. H., & Mason, R. O. (2004). The virtuous organization: The value of happiness in the workplace. *Organizational Dynamics, 33*(4), 379-392.

4. Gavin, J. H., & Mason, R. O. (2004). The virtuous organization: The value of happiness in the workplace. *Organizational Dynamics, 33*(4), 379-392.

5. Gallup. (2014, August 29). *The "40-hour" workweek is actually longer – by seven hours: Full-time U.S. workers, on average, report working 47 hours weekly* [Graphs]. Retrieved from http://www.gallup.com/poll/175286/hour-workweek-actually-longer-seven-hours.aspx

6. Bruch, H., & Ghoshal, S. (2002). Beware the busy manager. *Harvard Business Review, 80*(2), 62-69.

7. Roosevelt, T. (1910, April 23). *Citizenship in a Republic.* Speech presented at the Sorbonne University in Paris, France.

CHAPTER 2: HOW WE GOT HERE

NO ONE TO BLAME BUT OURSELVES

1. Holloway, S. L., & Pimlott-Wilson, H. (2014). Enriching children, institutionalizing childhood? Geographies of play, extracurricular activities, and parenting in England. *Annals of the Association of American Geographers, 104*(3), 613-627.

2. Schulte, B. (2013, November 6). Dads, too, want to have it all. *The Washington Post.* Retrieved from http://www.washingtonpost.com/blogs/she-the-people/wp/2013/11/06/dads-too-want-to-have-it-all/

3. Carpenter, M. C. (1992). Passionate kisses. On *Come on come on* [CD].
    Springfield, VA: Columbia Nashville.

4. Iyengar, S. S., & Lepper, M. R. (2000). When choice is demotivating: Can
    one desire too much of a good thing? *Journal of Personality and Social
    Psychology, 79*(6), 995-1006.

5. Smith, A. (1976). *An inquiry into the nature and causes of the wealth of
    nations.* Chicago, IL: Chicago University Press. (Original work published
    1793)

6. Smith, A. (1976). *An inquiry into the nature and causes of the wealth of
    nations.* Chicago, IL: Chicago University Press. (Original work published
    1793)

7. Przybylski, A. K., Murayama, K., DeHaan, C. R., & Gladwell, V. (2013).
    Motivational, emotional, and behavioral correlates of fear of missing out.
    Computers in Human Behavior, 29(4), 1841-1848.

8. Liedtke, M. (2013, May 28). Atari founder Nolan Bushnell talks about
    working with Steve Jobs in new book. *Huffington Post.* Retrieved from http://
    www.huffingtonpost.com/2013/03/28/nolan-bushnell-book_n_2966219.
    html

9. Simon, D. (2010, June 24). The gambling man who co-founded
    Apple and left for $800. *CNN.com.* Retrieved from http://edition.
    cnn.com/2010/TECH/web/06/24/apple.forgotten.founder/index.
    html?hpt=C1&fbid=lG95iTlU4iD

10. Kerly, D., & Dolak, K. (2012, January 31). Causes founder's $400M
    Facebook 'mistake'. *ABC News.* Retrieved from http://abcnews.go.com/US/
    founders-400m-facebook-mistake/story?id=15469445

11. Bessemer Venture Partners. (2015). Anti-portfolio. *Bessemer Venture
    Partners.* Retrieved from http://www.bvp.com/portfolio/antiportfolio

12. Altucher, J. (2011, March 10). 10 unusual things I didn't know about Google
    (also: The worst venture capital decision in history) [Web log comment].
    Retrieved   from   http://www.jamesaltucher.com/2011/03/10-unusual-
    things-about-google/

13. Przybylski, A. K., Murayama, K., DeHaan, C. R., & Gladwell, V. (2013).
    Motivational, emotional, and behavioral correlates of fear of missing out.
    Computers in Human Behavior, 29(4), 1841-1848.

14. Baumeister, R. F., & Leary, M. R. (1995). The need to belong: Desire for interpersonal attachments as a fundamental human motivation. *Psychological Bulletin, 117*(3), 497-529.

15. Spreitzer, G., Sutcliffe, K., Dutton, J., Sonenshein, S., & Grant, A. M. (2005). A socially embedded model of thriving at work. *Organization Science, 16*(5), 537-562.

16. McKeown, G. (2014). *Essentialism.* New York, NY: Crown Business.

17. Covey, S. R. (1990). *The 7 habits of highly effective people: Powerful lessons in personal change.* New York, NY: Fireside by Simon & Schuster.

18. Weber, M. (1958). *The Protestant ethic and the spirit of capitalism.* New York, NY: Scribner.

19. Sullivan, N. (2015). Puritan work ethic: Definition, lesson & quiz. *Study. com.* Retrieved from http://study.com/academy/lesson/puritan-work-ethic-definition-lesson-quiz.html

20. Ackroyd, P., Chaucer, G., & Bantock, N. (2009). *The Canterbury tales.* London: Penguin Classics.

21. Bruch, H., & Ghoshal, S. (2002). Beware the busy manager. *Harvard Business Review, 80*(2), 62-69.

22. Hallowell, E. M. (2007). *Crazy busy: Overstretched, overbooked, and about to snap! Strategies for handling your fast-paced life.* New York, NY: Ballantine Books.

23. Brown, B. (2012). *Daring greatly.* New York, NY: Gotham Books.

24. Brown, B. (2012). *Daring greatly.* New York, NY: Gotham Books.

HOW WE CAN TAKE IT BACK

1. Arons, B. (n.d.). A review of the cocktail party effect. *MIT Media Lab.* Retrieved from http://xenia.media.mit.edu/~barons/html/cocktail.html

2. Adept [Def. 1]. (1968). *Webster's new twentieth century dictionary of the English language unabridged* (2nd ed.). New York, NY: The World Publishing Company.

CHAPTER 3: ACCEPT(THE ECONOMICS OF PERFORMING WITH INTENT)

1. Cordova, J. V. (2001). Acceptance in behavior therapy: Understanding the process of change. *The Behavior Analyst, 24*, 213-226.

2. Irvine, W. B. (2006). *On desire.* New York, NY: Oxford University Press.

THE THREE ECONOMIC LAWS OF PERFORMING WITH INTENT

1. Ferdman, R. A. (2014, November 15). The world's biggest chocolate-maker says we're running out of chocolate. *The Washington Post*. Retrieved from http://www.washingtonpost.com/blogs/wonkblog/wp/2014/11/15/the-worlds-biggest-chocolate-maker-says-were-running-out-of-chocolate/

1. SUPPLY IS FINITE

1. Shiv, B., & Fedorikhin, A. (1999). Heart and mind in conflict: The interplay of affect and cognition in consumer decision making. *Journal of Consumer Research, 26*(3), 278-292.

2. U.S. Bureau of Labor Statistics. (2014, June 18). *American time use survey—2013 results.* Washington, D.C.: U.S. Bureau of Labor Statistics. Retrieved from http://www.bls.gov/tus/

3. Schabner, D. (2014, May 1). Americans work more than anyone. *ABCNews. com*. Retrieved from http://abcnews.go.com/US/story?id=93364

4. Schor, J. (1991). *The overworked American.* New York, NY: Basic Books.

5. U.S. Bureau of Labor Statistics. (2014, June 18). *American time use survey—2013 results.* Washington, D.C.: U.S. Bureau of Labor Statistics. Retrieved from http://www.bls.gov/tus/

6. U.S. Bureau of Labor Statistics. (2014, June 18). *American time use survey—2013 results.* Washington, D.C.: U.S. Bureau of Labor Statistics. Retrieved from http://www.bls.gov/tus/

2. DEMAND IS INFINITE

1. Harrison, Y., & Horne, J. A. (1999). One night of sleep loss impairs innovative thinking and flexible decision making. *Organizational Behavior and Human Decision Processes, 78*(2), 128-45.

2. Alhola, P., & Polo-Kantola, P. (2007). Sleep deprivation: Impact on cognitive performance. *Neuropsychiatric Disease and Treatment, 3*(5), 553–567.

3. Right Management. (2012, October 16). *Just one-in-five employees take actual lunch break.* Retrieved from https://www.right.com/news-and-events/press-releases/2012-press-releases/item23943.aspx

4. Biswas, A., Oh, P. I., Faulkner, G. E., Bajaj, R. R., Silver, M. A., Mitchell, M. S., & Alter, D. A. (2015). Sedentary time and its association with risk for disease incidence, mortality, and hospitalization in adults: A systematic review and meta-analysis. *Annals of Internal Medicine, 162*, 123-132.

5. Sommer, W., Stürmer, B., Shmuilovich, O., Martin-Loeches, M., & Schacht, A. (2013). How about lunch? Consequences of the meal context on cognition and emotion. *PLoS ONE 8*(7), 1-7.

6. Trougakos, J. P., Beal, D. J., Green, S. G., & Weiss, H. M. (2008). Making the break count: An episodic examination of recovery activities, emotional experiences, and positive affective displays. *Academy of Management Journal, 51*(1) 131-146.

7. Aspinall, P., Mavros, P., Coyne, R., & Roe, J. (2015). The urban brain: Analysing outdoor physical activity with mobile EEG. *British Journal of Sports Medicine, 49*(4), 272-276.

8. Zawadzki, M. J., Smyth, J. M., & Costigan, H. J. (2015). Real-time associations between engaging in leisure and daily health and well-being. *Annals of Behavioral Medicine.* Retrieved from http://www.ucmerced.edu/sites/ucmerced.edu/files/documents/zawadzki-paper-2015.pdf

9. U.S. Bureau of Labor Statistics. (2014, June 18). *American time use survey —2013 results.* Washington, D.C.: U.S. Bureau of Labor Statistics. Retrieved from http://www.bls.gov/tus/

3. RESOURCES MUST BE ALLOCATED WISELY

1. Fich, E. M. & Shivdasani, A. (2006). Are busy boards effective monitors? *The Journal of Finance, 61*(2), 689-724. Retrieved from http://onlinelibrary.wiley.com/doi/10.1111/j.1540-6261.2006.00852.x/full

2. Ramsey, D. (2003). *The total money makeover.* Nashville, TN: Nelson Books.

CHAPTER 4: DISCOVER (WHAT REALLY MATTERS)

1. Sinek, S. (2011). *Start with why: How great leaders inspire everyone to take action.* New York, NY: Penguin.

2. Colson, C., Gardner, D., Kleiner, J., & Winfrey, O. (Producers), & DuVernay, A. (Director). (2014). *Selma* [Motion picture]. United States: Paramount Pictures.

YOU CREATE YOUR OWN PURPOSE AND MEANING

1. Camus, A. (1991). *The myth of Sisyphus, and other essays.* New York, NY: Vintage Books.

2. Frankl, V. E. (2006). *Man's search for meaning* (4th ed.). Boston, MA: Beacon.

3. Forstarter, M., & White, M. (Producers), & Gilliam, T., & Jones, T. (Directors). (1975). *Monty Python and the Holy Grail* [Motion picture]. United Kingdom: Columbia Pictures.

WHY MEANING IS SO IMPORTANT

1. Frankl, V. (1978). *The unheard cry for meaning.* New York, NY: Simon & Schuster.

2. Bruner, J. (1990). Acts of meaning. Cambridge, MA: Harvard University Press.

3. Frankl, V. E. (1988). *The will to meaning: Foundations and applications of logotherapy.* New York, NY: Meridian.

4. Marshall, M., & Marshall, E. (2012, August 4). Logotherapy revisited: Review of the tenets of Viktor E. Frankl's logotherapy. Ottawa Institute of Logotherapy.

5. Frankl, V. E. (1988). *The will to meaning: Foundations and applications of logotherapy.* New York, NY: Meridian.

THE FIVE STEPS TO DISTILLING PRIORITIES

1. Potable [Def. 1]. (1968). *Webster's new twentieth century dictionary of the English language unabridged* (2nd ed.). New York, NY: The World Publishing Company.

1. GUIDING PRINCIPLES

1. Carville, J., & Begal, P. (2002). *Buck up, suck up...and come back when you foul up: 12 winning secrets from the war room.* New York, NY: Simon & Schuster.

2. Issues we care about (n.d.). In *Ben & Jerry's ice cream: Values.* Retrieved from http://www.benjerry.com/values/issues-we-care-about

3. Sachtman, T. (2007). *Runspringa: To be or not to be Amish.* New York, NY: North Point Press.

2. PASSION

1. Reeve, J., Deci, E. L., & Ryan, R. M. (2004). Self-determination theory: A dialectical framework for understanding sociocultural influences on student motivation. In D. McInerney, & S. Van Etten (Eds.). *Big theories revisited: Volume 4 in: Research on sociocultural influences on motivation and learning.* Information Age Publishing: Greenwich, CT.

2. Deci, E. L., & Ryan, R. M. (2002). Overview of self-determination theory: An organismic dialectical perspective. In E. Deci, & R. Ryan. (Eds.), *Handbook of self-determination research.* Rochester, NY: The University of Rochester Press.

3. McClelland, D. C. (1961). *The achieving society.* Princeton, NJ: Van Nostrand.

4. McClelland, D. C. (1971). *Assessing human motivation.* New York: General Learning Press.

5. Deci, E. L., & Ryan, R. M. (1985). *Intrinsic motivation and self-determination in human behavior.* New York, NY: Plenum Press.

6. Deci, E. L., & Ryan, R. M. (1985). *Intrinsic motivation and self-determination in human behavior.* New York, NY: Plenum Press.

7. Deci, E. L., & Ryan, R. M. (1985). *Intrinsic motivation and self-determination in human behavior.* New York, NY: Plenum Press.

8. Baumeister, R. F., & Leary, M. R. (1995). The need to belong: Desire for interpersonal attachments as a fundamental human motivation. *Psychological Bulletin, 117*(3), 497-529.

9. McClelland, D. C. (1971). *Assessing human motivation.* New York: General Learning Press.

10. Hill, J. B. (2000). *The legacy of luna: The story of a tree, a woman and the struggle to save the redwoods*. New York, NY: HarperCollins.

11. Crowther, T. W., Glick, H. B., Covey, K. R., Bettigole, C., Maynard, D. S., Thomas, S. M., Smith, J. R., Hintler, G., Duguid, M. C., Amatulli, G., Tuanmu, M.-N., Jetz, W., Salas, C., Stam, C., Piotto, D., Tavani, R., Green, S., Bruce, G., Williams, S. J., Wiser, S. K., Huber, M. O., Hengeveld, G. M., Nabuurs, G.-J., Tikhonova, E., Borchardt, P., Li, C.-F., Powrie, L. W., Fischer, M., Hemp, A., Homeier, J., Cho, P., Vibrans, A. C., Umunay, P. M., Piao, S. L., Rowe, C. W., Ashton, M. S., Crane, P. R., & Bradford, M. A. (2015, September 10). Mapping tree density at a global scale. *Nature, 525*, 201-205.

3. STRENGTHS AND WEAKNESSES

1. Rath, T. (2001). *StrengthsFinder 2.0: Discover what makes you stand out*. New York, NY: Gallup Press.

4. SUPPORT FROM OTHERS

1. Campbell, A., & Alexander, M. (1997). What's wrong with strategy? *Harvard Business Review, 75*(6), 42-51.

2. Hill, J. B. (2000). *The legacy of luna: The story of a tree, a woman and the struggle to save the redwoods*. New York, NY: HarperCollins.

3. Pfeffer, J., & Salancik, G. (1978). *The external control organizations: A resource dependence perspective*. New York, NY: Harper & Row.

5. SUPPORTING INFRASTRUCTURE

1. Carew, D. G., & Mandel, M. (2014). Infrastructure investment and economic growth: Surveying new post-crisis evidence. *Progressive Policy Institute*. Received from http://www.progressivepolicy.org/wp-content/uploads/2014/03/2014.03-Carew_Mandel_Infrastructure-Investment-and-Economic-Growth_Surveying-New-Post-Crisis-Evidence.pdf

2. National Institute on Drug Abuse. (2012, November). DrugFacts: Understanding drug abuse and addiction. *National Institute on Drug Abuse: The Science of Drug Abuse & Addiction*. Retrieved from http://www.drugabuse.gov/publications/drugfacts/understanding-drug-abuse-addiction

CHAPTER 5: ELIMINATE (WHAT DOESN'T MATTER)

1. Quiller-Couch, A. (1916). *On the art of writing: Lectures delivered in the University of Cambridge*, 1913-1914. Cambridge: University Press.

2. King, S. (2000). *On writing: A memoir of the craft.* New York, NY: Scribner.

RECOGNIZE

1. Kahneman, D., & Tversky, A. (1979). Prospect theory: An analysis of decision under risk. *Econometrica, 47*(2), 263-291.

2. Arkes, H. A., & Blummer, C. (1985). The psychology of sunk cost. *Organizational Behavior and Human Decision Processes, 35*(1), 124-140.

3. Frederick, S. (2011). The persuasive power of opportunity costs. *Harvard Business Review, 89*(1/2), 38-38.

4. Sinoway, E. C. (2012). No, you can't have it all. *Harvard Business Review, 90*(10), 111-114.

5. Eisenhower, D. D. (1953). The chance for peace. *Address Delivered Before the American Society of Newspaper Editors.* Retrieved from http://www.eisenhower.archives.gov/all_about_ike/speeches/chance_for_peace.pdf

6. Kahneman, D., Knetsch, J. L., & Thaler, R. H. (1991). Anomalies: The endowment effect, loss aversion, and status quo bias. *The Journal of Economic Perspectives, 5*(1), 193-206.

7. Kahneman, D., Knetsch, J. L., & Thaler, R. H. (1991). Anomalies: The endowment effect, loss aversion, and status quo bias. *The Journal of Economic Perspectives, 5*(1), 193-206.

RESIGN

1. Parker, P. (2011, December 16). *The fear of missing out: Priya Parker at tedxcambridge 2011* [Video file]. Retrieved from https://www.youtube.com/watch?v=P6w7Eq7YhL8

TAKE CHARGE

1. Pittenger, D. J., & Pavlik, W. B. (1988). Analysis of the partial reinforcement extinction effect in humans using absolute and relative comparisons of schedules. *American Journal of Psychology, 101*(1), 1-14.

2. Kusurkar, R. A., Croiset, G., & Ten Cate, O. T. (2011). Twelve tips to stimulate intrinsic motivation in students through autonomy-supportive classroom teaching derived from self-determination theory. *Medical Teacher, 33*(12), 978-982.

3. Klingberg, T. (2009). *The overflowing brain: Information overload and the limits of working memory.* New York, NY: Oxford University Press.

4. Medina, J. (2008). *Brain rules: 12 principles for surviving and thriving at work, home, and school.* Seattle, WA: Pear Press.

5. Toma, C. L., & Hancock, J. T. (2013). Self-affirmation underlies Facebook use. *Personality and Social Psychology Bulletin, 39*(3), 321-331.

6. Heath, C., & Heath, D. (2010). *Switch: How to change things when change is hard.* New York, NY: Crown Publishing.

7. McKeown, G. (2014). *Essentialism.* New York, NY: Crown Business.

8. McKeown, G. (2014). *Essentialism.* New York, NY: Crown Business.

9. Covey, S. R. (1990). *The 7 habits of highly effective people: Powerful lessons in personal change.* New York, NY: Fireside by Simon & Schuster.

10. Meltzer, H. (Producer), & Benjamin, R. (Director). (1998). *The pentagon wars* [Motion picture]. United States: HBO.

11. Guadagno, R. E., Asher, E., Demaine, L. J., & Cialdini, R. B. (2001). When saying yes leads to saying no: Preference for consistency and the reverse foot-in-the-door effect. *Personality and Social Psychology Bulletin, 27*(7), 859-867.

ELIMINATE AND PRIORITIZE

1. Lencioni, P. (2012). *The advantage: Why organizational health trumps everything else in business.* San Francisco, CA: Jossey-Bass.

2. Covey, S. R., Merrill, A. R., & Merrill, R. R. (1996). *First things first: To live, to love to learn, to leave a legacy.* New York, NY: Fireside by Simon & Schuster.

3. Keller, G., & Papasan, J. (2012). *The one thing: The surprisingly simple truth behind extraordinary results.* Austin, TX: Bard Press.

CHAPTER 6: PLAN (WHAT MATTERS)

1. Brinckmann, J., Grichnik, D., & Kapsa, D. (2010). Should entrepreneurs plan or just storm the castle? A meta-analysis on contextual factors impacting the business planning–performance relationship in small firms. *Journal of Business Venturing, 25*(1), 24-40.

MAPPING THE JOURNEY

1. Muehrcke, P. C., & Muehrcke, J. O. (1974). Maps in literature. *Geographical Review, 64*(3), 317-338.

2. Keller, G., & Papasan, J. (2012). *The one thing: The surprisingly simple truth behind extraordinary results.* Austin, TX: Bard Press.

1. YOUR NORTH STAR – YOUR WHY

1. Ambrose, S. E. (1996). *Undaunted courage: Meriwether Lewis, Thomas Jefferson, and the opening of the American west.* New York, NY: Simon and Schuster.

2. Trump, D., & Schwartz, T. (1987). *Trump: The art of the deal.* New York, NY: Random House.

3. Boudreau, J. (2006, April 10). Q&A with Apple co-founder Steve Wozniak. *The Seattle Times.* Retrieved from http://old.seattletimes.com/html/businesstechnology/2002921742_btwozniak10.html

4. Collier, P., & Horowitz, D. (1976). *The Rockefellers: An American dynasty.* New York, NY: Holt, Rindhart and Winston.

2. YOUR PATH – YOUR HOW

1. Twain, M. (2001). *A Connecticut Yankee in King Arthur's court.* Mineola, NY: Dover Publications. (Original work published 1889)

3. YOUR DESTINATION – YOUR LONG-TERM OBJECTIVE

1. Doran, G. T. (1981). There's a S.M.A.R.T. way to write management's goals and objectives. *Management Review, 70*(11), 35-36.

2. Bos, P. V. (2010). How to set business goals. *Inc.* Retrieved from http://www.inc.com/guides/2010/06/setting-business-goals.html

4. YOUR MILESTONES – YOUR SHORT-TERM OBJECTIVES

1. Milestone Society. (n.d.). Milestones & waymarkers. *Milestone Society.* Retrieved from http://www.milestonesociety.co.uk/aboutmilestones.html

2. Covey, S. M. R., & Merrill, R. R. (2006). *The speed of trust: The one thing that changes everything.* New York, NY: Free Press.

3. Covey, S. M. R., & Merrill, R. R. (2006). *The speed of trust: The one thing that changes everything.* New York, NY: Free Press.

4. NASA. (n.d.). NASA history timeline. *NASA.* Retrieved from http://www. nasa.gov/50th/timeline.html

5. YOUR STEPS – YOUR PROGRESS INDICATORS

1. Amabile, T. M., & Kramer, S. J. (2011). *The progress principle: Using small wins to ignite joy, engagement, and creativity at work.* Boston, MA: Harvard Business Review Press.

2. Kivetz, R., Urminsky, O, & Zheng, Y. (2006). The goal-gradient hypothesis resurrected: Purchase acceleration, illusionary goal progress, and customer retention. *Journal of Marketing Research, 43*(1), 39-58.

3. Amabile, T. M., & Kramer, S. J. (2011). *The progress principle: Using small wins to ignite joy, engagement, and creativity at work.* Boston, MA: Harvard Business Review Press.

PUTTING IT ALL TOGETHER

1. National Archives. (n.d.). A history of naval deck logs. *National Archives.* Retrieved from http://www.archives.gov/research/military/logbooks/ naval-deck-logs.html

2. Boud, D. (2001). Using journal writing to enhance reflective practice. In L. M. English & M. A. Gillen (Eds.), *Promoting journal writing in adult education: New directions for adult and continuing education, No. 90* (pp. 9-17). San Francisco, CA: Jossey-Bass.

3. Fulwiler, T. (1987). *The journal book.* Portsmouth, NH: Heinemann.

4. Moon, J. A. (2006). *Learning journals: A handbook for academics, students and professional development* (2nd ed.). London: Kogan Page.

5. Stevens, D. D., & Cooper, J. E. (2009). *Journal keeping: How to use reflective writing for learning, teaching, professional insight, and positive change.* Sterling, VA: Stylus.

6. Burka, J. B., & Yuen, L. M. (2008). *Procrastination: Why you do it, what to do about it.* New York: NY: Da Capo Lifelong Books.

7. Bruch, H., & Ghoshal, S. (2002). Beware the busy manager. *Harvard Business Review, 80*(2), 62-69.

8. Steel, P. (2007). The nature of procrastination: A meta-analytic and theoretical review of quintessential self-regulatory failure. *Psychological Bulletin, 133*(1), 65-94.

9. Steel, P. (2007). The nature of procrastination: A meta-analytic and theoretical review of quintessential self-regulatory failure. *Psychological Bulletin, 133*(1), 65-94.

10. Palladino, L. J. (2007). *Find your focus zone: An effective new plan to defeat distraction and overload.* New York, NY: Free Press by Simon & Schuster.

11. Schiffbauer, L. W. (2013). *The pursuit of self-esteem: A help or a hindrance in thriving in the workplace?* (Doctoral dissertation). Retrieved from ProQuest, UMI Dissertations Publishing. (UMI 3596255)

12. Keller, G., & Papasan, J. (2012). *The one thing: The surprisingly simple truth behind extraordinary results.* Austin, TX: Bard Press.

13. Keller, G., & Papasan, J. (2012). *The one thing: The surprisingly simple truth behind extraordinary results.* Austin, TX: Bard Press.

CHAPTER 7 TAKE ACTION (WITH INTENT)

1. Glen Canyon National Recreation Area. (n.d.). Hole-in-the-rock. *National Park Service.* Retrieved from http://www.nps.gov/glca/learn/historyculture/holeintherock.htm

1. CREATE PURPOSEFUL HABITS

1. Duhigg, C. (2014).*The power of habit: Why we do what we do in life and business.* New York, NY: Random House.

2. Dweck, C. S. (2010). *Succeed: How we can reach our goals.* New York, NY: Hudson Street Press.

3. Fogg, B. J. (2012, December 5). *Forget big change, start with a tiny habit: BJ Fogg at TEDxFremont* [Video file]. Retrieved from https://www.youtube.com/watch?v=AdKUJxjn-R8

2. SCHEDULE A BUFFER

1. Kahneman, D., & Tversky, A. (1979). Intuitive prediction: Biases and corrective procedures. *TIMS Studies in Management Science, 12*, 313-327.

3. KEEP YOUR SUPPORTERS CHEERING

1. Dalai Lama, & Cutler, H. C. (1998). *The art of happiness.* New York, NY: Riverhead Books.

2. Bateman, T. S., & Snell, S. A. (2011). *Management: Leading & collaborating in a competitive world* (9th ed.). New York, NY: McGraw-Hill Irwin.

3. Jick, T. D. (2003). *Managing change: Cases and concepts* (2nd ed.). New York, NY: Irwin Publishing.

4. ABANDON THE MYTH OF MULTITASKING

1. American Psychological Association. (2006, March 20). Multitasking: Switching costs. *American Psychological Association.* Retrieved from http://www.apa.org/research/action/multitask.aspx

2. Rubinstein, J. S., Meyer, D. E. & Evans, J. E. (2001). Executive control of cognitive processes in task switching. *Journal of Experimental Psychology: Human Perception and Performance, 27*(4), 763-797.

3. Yeung, N. & Monsell, S. (2003). Switching between tasks of unequal familiarity: The role of stimulus-attribute and response-set selection. *Journal of Experimental Psychology-Human Perception and Performance, 29*(2), 455-469.

4. Hembrooke, H., & Gay, G. (2003). The laptop and the lecture: The effects of multitasking in learning environments. *Journal of Computing in Higher Education, 15*(1), 46-64.

5. Meyer, D. E. & Kieras, D. E. (1997a). A computational theory of executive cognitive processes and multiple-task performance: Part 1. Basic mechanisms. *Psychological Review, 104*, 3-65.

6. Meyer, D. E. & Kieras, D. E. (1997b). A computational theory of executive cognitive processes and multiple-task performance: Part 2. Accounts of psychological refractory-period phenomena. *Psychological Review, 104*, 749-791.

7. Mark, G. M., Voida, S., & Cardello, A. V. (2012). "A pace not dictated by electrons": An empirical study of work without email. In *Proceedings of the SIGCHI Conference on Human Factors in Computing Systems* (CHI 2012, pp. 555–564), Austin, Texas, May 5-10.

8. Strayer, D. L., Drews, F. A., & Crouch, D. J. (2006). A comparison of the cell phone driver and the drunk driver. *Human Factors: The Journal of the Human Factors and Ergonomics Society, 48*, 381-391.

9. Drews, F. A., Pasupathi, M., & Strayer, D. L. (2008). Passenger and cell phone conversations in simulated driving. *Journal of Experimental Psychology: Applied, 14*(4), 392-400.

10. Ophir, E., Nass, C., & Wagner, A. D. (2009). Cognitive control in media multitaskers. *Proceedings of the National Academy of Sciences, 106*(37), 15583-15587.

11. Pennebaker, R. (2009, August 29). The mediocre multitasker. *The New York Times.* Retrieved from http://www.nytimes.com/2009/08/30/weekinreview/30pennebaker.html#

12. Ophir, E., Nass, C., & Wagner, A. D. (2009). Cognitive control in media multitaskers. *Proceedings of the National Academy of Sciences, 106*(37), 15583-15587.

13. Ophir, E., Nass, C., & Wagner, A. D. (2009). Cognitive control in media multitaskers. *Proceedings of the National Academy of Sciences, 106*(37), 15583-15587.

14. Csikszentmihalyi, M. (1990). *Flow: The psychology of optimal experience.* New York, NY: Harper Collins.

5. STRIVE FOR PROGRESS; NOT PERFECTION

1. Chang, E. C. (2000). Perfectionism as a predictor of positive and negative psychological outcomes: Examining a mediation model in younger and older adults. *Journal of Counseling Psychology, 47*(1), 18-26.

2. Kawamura, K. Y., Hunt, S. L., Frost, R. O., & DiBartolo, P. M. (2001). Perfectionism, anxiety, and depression: Are the relationships independent? *Cognitive Therapy and Research, 25*(3), 291-301.

3. O'Connor, R. C., & O'Connor, D. B. (2003). Predicting hopelessness and psychological distress: The role of perfectionism and coping. *Journal of Counseling Psychology, 50*(3), 362-372.

6. EMBRACE THE SERENITY PRAYER

1. Shapiro, F. R. (2008, July/August). Who wrote the serenity prayer: The inspiring text—long attributed to an eminent theologian—may have deeper roots than we thought. *Yale Alumni Magazine*. Retrieved from http://archives.yalealumnimagazine.com/issues/2008_07/serenity.html

2. Zimbardo, P. G. (1985). *Psychology and life*. Glenview, IL: Scott Foresman.

3. Cherry, K. (2015). What is your locus of control? Are you in control of your destiny? *Psychology.about.com*. Retrieved from http://psychology.about.com/od/personalitydevelopment/fl/What-Is-Locus-of-Control.htm

4. Ngwoke, D. U., Oyeoku, E. K., & Obikwelu, C. L. (2013). Perceived locus of control as a predictor of entrepreneurial development and job creation among students in the tertiary institution. *Journal of Education and Practice, 4*(14), 49-54.

5. Martin, R. (2015, July 1.) Freedom to marry founder: 'The day of the gay exception is over'. *NPR*. Retrieved from http://www.npr.org/2015/06/26/417840292/freedom-to-marry-founder-the-day-of-the-gay-exception-is-over

6. Braw, E. (2014, September 29). The three letter word driving a gender revolution. *Newsweek*. Retrieved from http://www.newsweek.com/2014/10/03/three-letter-word-driving-gender-revolution-272654.html

7. Neuman, S. (2015, March 27.) He, she, or hen? Sweden's new gender-neutral pronoun. *NPR*. Retrieved from http://www.npr.org/blogs/thetwo-way/2015/03/27/395785965/he-she-or-hen-sweden-s-new-gender-neutral-pronoun

7. LEARN FROM YOUR FAILURES

1. Edmondson, A. C. (2011, April). *Strategies for learning from failure* [Video file]. Retrieved from https://hbr.org/2011/04/strategies-for-learning-from-failure

1. Edmondson, A. C. (2011, April). *Strategies for learning from failure* [Video file]. Retrieved from https://hbr.org/2011/04/strategies-for-learning-from-failure

2. Forbes, B. C. (1921, January). Why do so many men never amount to anything? *American Magazine, 91*, 89.

1. Edmondson, A. C. (2011, April). *Strategies for learning from failure* [Video file]. Retrieved from https://hbr.org/2011/04/strategies-for-learning-from-failure

2. Myers, C. G., Staats, B. R., & Gino, F. (2014). *"My bad!" How internal attribution and ambiguity of responsibility affect learning from failure* (No. 14-104). HBS Working Paper. Retrieved from http://www.hbs.edu/faculty/Publication percent20Files/14-104_59aab8f4-6050-403c-bb0e-c91728b95f02.pdf

1. Edmondson, A. C. (2011, April). *Strategies for learning from failure* [Video file]. Retrieved from https://hbr.org/2011/04/strategies-for-learning-from-failure

2. Coelho, P. R. P., & McClure, J. E. (2005). Learning from failure. *Mid-American Journal of Business, 20*(1), 1.

3. Kaufman, S. B. (2009, January 21). Learning about learning: An interview with Joshua Waitzkin. *SharpBrains.com*. Retrieved from http://sharpbrains.com/blog/2009/01/21/learning-about-learning-an-interview-with-joshua-waitzkin/

4. Briceno, E. (2012, November 18). *The power of belief—Mindset and success* [Video file]. Retrieved from https://www.youtube.com/watch?v=pN34FNbOKXc

8. BEWARE OF OVERLOAD AND ANXIETY

1. Hallowell, E. (2005, January). Overloaded circuits: Why smart people underperform. *Harvard Business Review*.

2. Hallowell, E. (2005, January). Overloaded circuits: Why smart people underperform. *Harvard Business Review*.

3. Whitney, P., Hinson, J. M., Jackson, M. L., & Van Dongen, H. P. (2015). Feedback blunting: Total sleep deprivation impairs decision making that requires updating based on feedback. *Sleep, 38*(5), 745-754.

4. Singh, M. (2015, May 12). Short on sleep? You could be a disaster waiting to happen. *NPR.* Retrieved from http://www.npr.org/sections/health-shots/2015/05/12/406137352/short-on-sleep-you-could-be-a-disaster-waiting-to-happen

5. M. S., & Alter, D. A. (2015). Sedentary time and its association with risk for disease incidence, mortality, and hospitalization in adults: A systematic review and meta-analysis. *Annals of Internal Medicine, 162*, 123-132.

6. Sommer, W., Stürmer, B., Shmuilovich, O., Martin-Loeches, M., & Schacht, A. (2013). How about lunch? Consequences of the meal context on cognition and emotion. *PLoS ONE 8*(7), 1-7.

7. Hogan, C. L., Mata, J., & Carstensen, L. L. (2013). Exercise holds immediate benefits for affect and cognition in younger and older adults. *Psychology and Aging, 28*(2), 587-594.

8. Aspinall, P., Mavros, P., Coyne, R., & Roe, J. (2015). The urban brain: Analysing outdoor physical activity with mobile EEG. *British Journal of Sports Medicine, 49*(4), 272-276.

9. Goldberg, J. (2014, June 24). The effects of stress on your body. *WebMD.* Retrieved from http://www.webmd.com/balance/stress-management/effects-of-stress-on-your-body#1

10. McGonigal, K. (2013, June). *How to make stress your friend* [Video file]. Retrieved from https://www.ted.com/talks/kelly_mcgonigal_how_to_make_stress_your_friend?language=en

11. McGonigal, K. (2013, June). *How to make stress your friend* [Video file]. Retrieved from https://www.ted.com/talks/kelly_mcgonigal_how_to_make_stress_your_friend?language=en

12. McGonigal, K. (2013, June). *How to make stress your friend* [Video file]. Retrieved from https://www.ted.com/talks/kelly_mcgonigal_how_to_make_stress_your_friend?language=en

9. KEEP IT ALL IN PERSPECTIVE

1. Crocker, J., & Wolfe, C. T. (2001). Contingencies of self-worth. *Psychological Review, 108*(3), 593-623.

2. Bangs, L. (Producer), & Bangs, L. (Director). (2013). *Marc Maron: Thinky pain* [TV Special]. United States: Netflix.

10. ENJOY THE JOURNEY

1. Campbell, J. (1968). *The hero with a thousand faces.* Princeton, NJ: Princeton University Press.

2. Konner, J., & Perlmutter, A. H. (Producers). (1988). *The power of myth* [Television series]. Arlington, VA: Public Broadcasting Service.

3. Larsen, S., & Larsen, R. (2002). *Joseph Campbell: A fire in the mind.* Rochester, VT: Inner Traditions.

About the Author

Lon Schiffbauer is an Assistant Professor of Business Management at Salt Lake Community College and Research Director with Vivifi, a business strategy consulting firm dedicated to helping companies develop thriving organizational cultures. In addition to his academic and consulting background, Lon has over 25 years' experience working for such companies as FedEx, Intel, and eBay, as well as a variety of small to mid-sized companies around the world. Lon holds an MBA and a Ph.D. in Industrial/Organizational Psychology. For his doctoral dissertation he studied the effects of the pursuit of self-esteem on an employee's ability to thrive in the workplace. He is also SPHR certified with the Society for Human Resource Management. Lon grew up in Palo Alto, CA, then went on to study and work in England, France, Japan, and Malaysia before settling in Sandy, Utah.

Over the years Lon has accomplished many of his life's goals by using the principles included in this book. Together with his wife of close to 30 years Lon raised a family of five kids, earned several university degrees and certifications, and completed dozens of endurance sporting events; Ironman races, marathons, and century bike rides. With the help of his business partner, Lon started a successful consulting firm that supported clients all over the world. He also wrote several books and successfully transitioned his career from the corporate to the academic arena. Throughout all this, Lon maintained a healthy balance in his life by focusing his efforts on what mattered most at the time.

(Then again, he still has a disassembled '65 MG Midget in his garage and countless unfinished books, so the guy still has a thing or two to learn.)

CPSIA information can be obtained
at www.ICGtesting.com
Printed in the USA
FSHW010607271218
54710FS